THE PLAY'S THE THING

A Whole Language Approach to Learning English

THE PLAY'S THE THING

A Whole Language Approach to Learning English

Valerie Whiteson
Evergreen Valley College

Nava Horovitz
Talpiot Teachers College

St. Martin's Press
New York

Editorial director, ESL/ELT: Tina B. Carver
Assistant editor: Kimberly Wurtzel
Manager, Publishing services: Emily Berleth
Assistant editor, Publishing services: Meryl Gross
Project management: Books By Design, Inc.
Production supervisor: Scott Lavelle
Text design: Books By Design, Inc.
Cover design: Evelyn Horovicz
Cover art: © Sean Kane/SIS

Library of Congress Catalog Card Number: 97-66121

Manufactured in the United States of America

3 2 1 0 9 8
f e d c b a

For information, write:

    St. Martin's Press, Inc.
    175 Fifth Avenue
    New York, NY 10010

ISBN: 0-312-15452-6

Acknowledgments

Photo credits: p. 3: Courtesy of Cameri Theatre; p. 15: Courtesy of San Jose Rep. Photo: P. Kirk; p. 25: Courtesy of Photofest. Photo: T. Charles Erickson; p. 37: Martha Swope © Time Inc.; p. 49: Courtesy of San Jose Rep. Photo: Wilson P. Graham; p. 65: Courtesy of Haramati Photographers; p. 75: Courtesy of Photofest. Photo: Bill Doll & Company; p. 87: Courtesy of Haramati Photographers; p. 97: Courtesy of Haramati Photographers; p. 109: Courtesy of Haramati Photographers; p. 121: Courtesy of Haramati Photographers; p. 131: Courtesy of San Jose Rep. Photo: Wilson P. Graham; p. 141: Courtesy of Haramati Photographers; p. 155: Courtesy of Photofest

Jane Anderson. Excerpt from *The Baby Dance.* Copyright ©1992 by Jane Anderson. Reprinted by permission of Samuel French, Inc., Play Publishers and Authors' Representatives.

Shelagh Delaney. Excerpt from *A Taste of Honey.* Copyright ©1989 by Grove Press, Inc. Used by permission of Grove/Atlantic, Inc.

Maria Irene Fornes. Excerpt from *Mud.* ©1983 by Maria Irene Fornes. Reprinted by permission of The Johns Hopkins University Press.

Athol Fugard. Excerpt from *"Master Harold"... and the Boys* by Athol Fugard. Copyright ©1982 by Athol Fugard. Reprinted by permission of Alfred A. Knopf, Inc.

Acknowledgments and copyrights are continued on page xix, which constitutes an extension of the copyright page.

CONTENTS

UNIT 3   You Are What You Eat   24

UNIT 8   Will You Help Me Find a Job?   86

UNIT 9   Nature or Nurture?   96

UNIT 10 Do You Believe in Luck?   108

UNIT 11 Job Satisfaction   120

UNIT 12 Which Is More Important— the Past, Present, or Future? 130

UNIT 13 Arranging a Marriage 140

UNIT 14 The Greatest Person Who Ever Lived   154

Appendix   166

TO THE INSTRUCTOR

A major problem in teaching a new language is to match the content of the lessons to the intellectual and cognitive skills of the students. Too often, students at elementary levels are not stimulated or excited by the content of their lessons. For both native and second-language speakers, the whole language approach seeks to engage the learner through the reading of untampered texts, storytelling, student-generated writing, making social and personal connections to content, student choice and responsibility for learning, acceptance of errors, and, above all, a constant emphasis on meaning. We practice this approach by concentrating on real language, such as that found in literature.

While it is possible to find good examples of modern literature for more advanced students, it has been difficult to find good writing for less advanced students. One way of studying excellent writing is through drama. By offering carefully chosen scenes from plays, *The Play's the Thing* provides an opportunity for intermediate and lower-intermediate students to learn English while being exposed to genuine literature. The selections include highly engaging and accessible readings by ethnically diverse writers, both male and female, from around the world. They reflect the multicultural perspective of the ESL classroom.

Many students who began studying English in their home countries know only one style of speaking, which is often too formal for everyday discourse. Because they are rich in dialogue, plays encourage a focus on natural-sounding conversation. Of course, dramatic dialogue does differ in certain ways from ordinary conversation. It has been "tidied up" so as to omit most of the hesitations, incomplete ideas, and interruptions that occur in normal speech. Nevertheless, the writing of a good playwright can still serve as an excellent model for English speech.

Most good drama needs interpretation; one must move beyond the surface of the words to make sense of what is being said. By asking our students to do this, we are helping them to understand conversational discourse. They will learn "how conversations are ordered and sequenced in English, what kinds of formulaic expressions it is appropriate to use in different contexts, how what people say in conversation reflects their relationship and relative status" (Lazar, 1993, p. 137).

If the texts are read or performed in class, students pick up appropriate expressions and pay attention to pronunciation and body language. Teachers have found that acting out plays or skits is an ideal way to create cohesion and cooperation in a group. Students are involved and motivated because they are learning by participating. In addition, by dealing with real issues in their lives, plays encourage students to become emotionally and intellectually engaged on a deeper level. Ideally, students will share their own experiences and learn to empathize with others.

Students bring their own unique characteristics to the learning process and the culture of the school. In any group of learners, we face a variety of learning style differences that require multiple approaches to both content and process (Gardner, 1983).

The written text helps boost students' confidence by providing a basis from which to develop oral skills. This is a great advantage for shy or inhibited students who find participating in a role play too threatening. By performing short scenes, students can also concentrate on their body language, gestures, eye contact, and relative distance. All of these nonverbal elements can be compared with the way things are done in the students' original cultures.

The wide range of activities in *The Play's the Thing* provides practice in the four critical language skills: reading, writing, listening, and speaking. Introductory exercises prepare students for the topic in question. Comprehension questions help deepen the students' understanding of the texts. Discussion questions lead to lively interaction in the classroom. Topics for discussion and writing focus on issues that affect the students' lives, such as what it means to belong to a culture, or the differences between nature and nurture. The units will also focus on vocabulary and idiomatic phrases, or "language chunks," that are essential for spoken language.

Language functions such as agreeing, encouraging, and introducing are explained and practiced. Differences between the spoken and written styles are studied, with special advice for writing a good composition or paragraph in Unit 1. Prose passages, including letters, articles, and recipes, extend the range of reading experiences. Exercises are given for listening skills such as following directions, taking notes, and telephone conversations. The special assignments at the end of each unit provide an outlet for each student's creativity and imagination.

The activities in each unit give teachers multiple ways to assess proficiency in their students' English. The projects in the Writing Activities and Special Assignments sections can generate contributions to a portfolio. The teachers' guide offers advice on how students can keep a log and write journal entries about their reading experiences and how teachers can incorporate e-mail and the Internet into their lessons. The teachers' guide also gives suggestions about adapting activities to the diverse needs of a heterogeneous class.

The materials we use should enable acquisition via comprehensible input (Krashen, 1982). The scenes from the plays we have chosen do provide comprehensible input. We have not included traditional grammar explanations and exercises in this text, as we believe that such study is peripheral. (We do, however, include some explanations and exercises in an appendix for those teachers who require them.)

Students of English as a second or foreign language need help to understand texts. They require the kind of "scaffolding" described by theorists such as Vygotsky. We try to provide the students with this kind of help to allow them to achieve their goals.

By introducing students to playwrights from a variety of countries and cultures that have helped shape our world, we are giving them an opportunity to appreciate aspects of English culture that many may never find on their own. By introducing them to real English and real literature, we express our confidence in their ability to enjoy the best that English has to offer. Ultimately, we hope, some of the students will develop a love for English that will help to make it truly their other language.

The Play's the Thing program consists of the following components. The student textbook contains the scenes from the plays together with all the activities, exercises, and assignments for a complete course. The grammar section appears as an appendix. The amount of stress given to grammar in conjunction with the rest of the material will depend on the individual instructor, the requirements of the course, and the level of the class. The Instructor's Manual contains a section-by-section explanation of how to use the book, together with suggestions, instructions, and ideas for supplementary activities. An answer key to all the exercises is provided for the instructor, along with tapescripts of the "Listening Task" sections. The Audio Cassette contains dramatic recordings of the scenes from the plays. In addition, all the texts for the "Listening Task" sections are on the cassette.

REFERENCES

Gardner, H. 1983. *Frame of Mind.* New York: Basic Books.

Krashen, S. D. 1982. *Principles and Practice in Second Language Acquisition in the Classroom.* Oxford: Pergamon Press.

Lazar, Gillian. 1993. *Literature and Language Teaching.* Cambridge (U.K.): Cambridge University Press.

ACKNOWLEDGMENTS

We would like to thank the authors of the plays and other writings we have chosen for this book. We thank them for their ideas and wonderful words. We'd also like to thank the photographers whose pictures help make the characters of the plays come alive for the students. We encourage students to find opportunities to visit the theater. We'd like to thank the actors and technicians who produced the audiotape for their outstanding contributions. Thanks as well to the artists who produced the cover.

We are grateful to the high school and college teachers in the U.S. and Israel and to Lorraine McClelland of Evergreen Valley College who reviewed the materials and field-tested them with their students. Their suggestions, including the contributions of students in the Materials course at Bar Ilan University, were most helpful in revising and improving the book. Thank you, too, to the following reviewers for St. Martin's Press: Priscilla Karant, American Language Institute at NYU; Nadia

Scholnick, City College of San Francisco; Gregg Segal, University of Southern California Language Academy; Roberta G. Steinberg, Mount Ida College; and Susan L. Stern, Irvine Valley College.

Special thanks to the editors and publishers who believed in the project.

Valerie Whiteson
Nava Horovitz

ACKNOWLEDGMENTS *(continued from copyright page)*

David Henry Hwang. Excerpt from *FOB*. From *FOB and Other Stories* by David Henry Hwang. Copyright ©1990 by David Henry Hwang. Introduction and Foreword by Maxine Hong Kingston. Used by permission of Dutton Signet, a division of Penguin Books USA, Inc.

Henrik Ibsen. Excerpt from *A Doll's House* by Henrik Ibsen, translated by Michael Meyer. Copyright © 1966 by Michael Meyer; copyright renewed 1994 by Michael Meyer. Reprinted by permission of Harold Ober Associates Incorporated. CAUTION: These plays are fully protected, in whole, in part, or in any form under the copyright laws of the United States of America, the British Empire including the Dominion of Canada, and all other countries of the Copyright Union, and are subject to royalty. All rights including motion picture, radio, television, recitation, public reading are strictly reserved. For professional rights and amateur rights all inquiries should be addressed to the Author's agent: Robert A. Freedman Dramatic Agency, Inc., 1501 Broadway, New York, NY 10036.

Eugene Ionesco. Scene from "The Lesson" in *The Bald Soprano and Other Plays* by Eugene Ionesco, translated by Donald M. Allen. Copyright ©1958 by Grove Press, Inc. Used by permission of Grove/Atlantic, Inc.

Arthur Miller. Excerpt from *All My Sons*. Copyright ©1947; renewed 1975 by Arthur Miller. From *Arthur Miller's Collected Plays* by Arthur Miller. Used by permission of Viking Penguin, a division of Penguin Books USA, Inc. and Greene & Heaton Ltd.

Marsha Norman. Excerpt from *'night Mother*. Copyright ©1983 by Marsha Norman. Reprinted by permission of Hill and Wang, a division of Farrar, Straus & Giroux, Inc. CAUTION: Professionals and amateurs are hereby warned that *'night Mother* by Marsha Norman, being fully protected under the Copyright Laws of the United States of America and all other countries of the Berne and Universal Copyright Conventions, is subject to a royalty. All rights including, but not limited to, professional, amateur, recording, motion picture, recitation, lecturing, public reading, radio and television broadcasting, and the rights of translation into foreign languages are expressly reserved. All inquiries concerning rights (other than stock and amateur rights) should be addressed to author's agent, William Morris Agency, Attention: Samuel Schiff, 1350 Avenue of the Americas, New York, NY 10019. Stock and amateur production rights for these plays are controlled exclusively by Dramatists Play Service Inc., 440 Park Avenue South, New York, NY 10016. No stock or amateur performance of the play may be given without obtaining in advance the written permission of Dramatists Play Service Inc., and paying the requisite fees.

Harold Pinter. Excerpt from *The Dumb Waiter*. Copyright ©1960, 1988 by Harold Pinter. Used by permission of Grove Press, Inc. and Faber and Faber, Limited.

Gary Snyder. "Seaman's Ditty." From *Left Out in the Rain* by Gary Snyder. Copyright ©1986 by Gary Snyder. Reprinted by permission of North Point Press, a division of Farrar, Straus & Giroux, Inc.

Michael Tremblay. Excerpt from *La Maison Suspendue*. Copyright ©1990 Lemeac Editeur. Reprinted by permission of G. C. Goodwin & Associates.

Abigail Van Buren. "Dear Abby" letter. Copyright © Abigail Van Buren/Universal Press Syndicate. Reprinted by permission.

Alice Walker. Excerpts from *The Color Purple*. Copyright ©1982 by Alice Walker. Reprinted by permission of Harcourt Brace & Company and David Higham Associates.

Wendy Wasserstein. Excerpt from *Tender Offer*. First published in *Antaeus* 66, *Plays in One Act*, pp. 452–58. Copyright ©1991 by Wendy Wasserstein. No part of this material may be reproduced in whole or in part without the express written permission of the author or her agent. Reprinted by permission of Rosenstone/Wender.

August Wilson. Excerpt from *The Piano Lesson* by August Wilson. Copyright ©1988, 1990 by August Wilson. Used by permission of Dutton Signet, a division of Penguin Books USA, Inc.

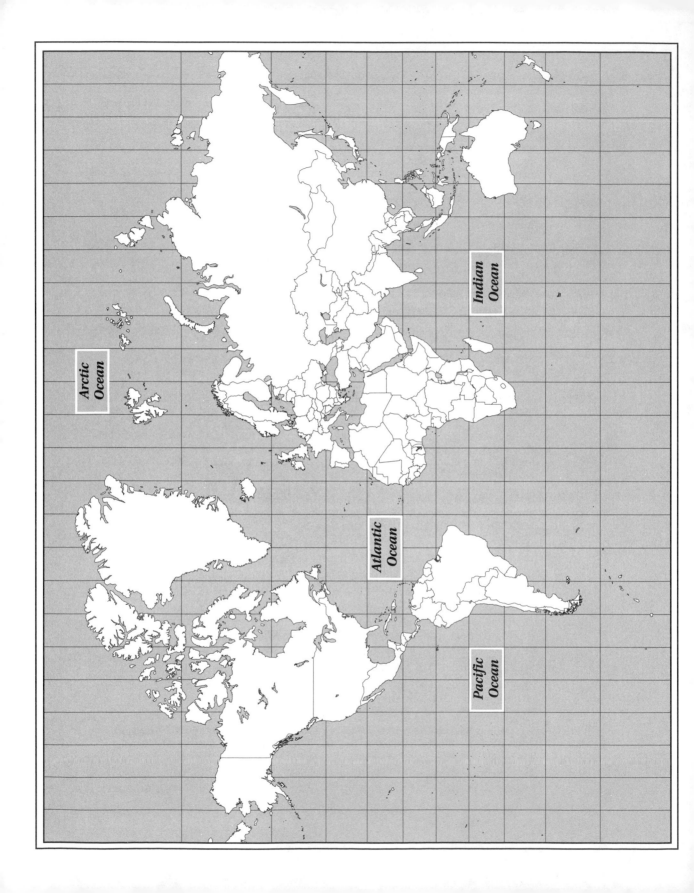

Introduction to Drama

Drama means "theatrical play or action." A play is different from a short story or a novel in that the characters are represented by actors. Playwrights, or the authors of the play, address their work to an audience, the people who see the play, and not especially to readers.

However, there are several advantages to reading a play. One is that you get to study it as an actor or director would. You can read it as slowly or as quickly as you like, and you can reread parts that you want to study more carefully. This is, more or less, what you will be doing with the excerpts from the plays that we have chosen. We also suggest that you try to act out the scenes yourselves.

Because you will be reading excerpts rather than the whole play, and you won't be seeing it on the stage where you would have the help of scenery, stage action, and the actors' tone of voice, you will have to study the texts carefully and read the playwright's directions and descriptions as well. These *stage directions* will give you important information about the characters and what is going on around them.

Plays today are different from those written hundreds of years ago, but they still have some things in common. Every play has *characters*, the imaginary people in the play; a *conflict*, which may be an argument between characters or a problem to be solved; and *suspense*, which keeps the audience wondering what will happen next or how the conflict will be resolved. The *plot* is the story of the play.

UNIT 1 How Do You Do?

INTRODUCTION

Here are some questions for you to think about and discuss:

Do you know how to introduce yourself to people?

What do you say when you first meet someone?

Does it matter whether the person is a teacher, a neighbor, or a classmate?

When you go into a strange person's house, do you know how to behave?

How do you get a conversation going?

What kinds of questions can you ask a stranger?

What kinds of questions shouldn't you ask?

What kinds of questions do you hate to reply to?

A B O U T   T H E   P L A Y

Eugene Ionesco was born in Romania in 1912 and was one of
Europe's most famous playwrights. Ionesco became a playwright
in a strange way. He wanted to learn English, and he studied a phrase
book to help him. He thought that many of the sentences in the book
sounded silly, so he wrote a nonsense play, *The Bald Soprano*, using sentences from the phrase book. It was a great success, and he went on to
write many other plays.

The play we are going to study was written in 1951 and translated into
English in 1958. In *The Lesson*, Ionesco introduces us to two characters:
a professor (age 50 to 60) and his young pupil (age 18), who is coming to

study with the professor. This is the first time they have met. The situation is very formal, and the language they use is too.

Ionesco uses tragedy and comedy to show us his view of the world. In *The Lesson*, the teacher shows the pupil how well he can use language to gain power over her.

Eugene Ionesco
from THE LESSON

Don't forget to read the stage directions,
shown in italics, as well as the dialogue.

PROFESSOR: Good morning, young lady. You . . . I expect that you . . . that you are the new pupil?

PUPIL: *(Turns quickly with a lively and self-assured manner; she gets up, goes toward the Professor, and gives him her hand.)* Yes, Professor. Good morning, Professor. As you see, I'm on time. I didn't want to be late.

PROFESSOR: That's fine, miss. Thank you, you didn't really need to hurry. I am very sorry to have kept you waiting . . . I was just finishing up . . . well . . . I'm sorry . . . You will excuse me, won't you? . . .

PUPIL: Oh, certainly, Professor. It doesn't matter at all, Professor.

PROFESSOR: Please excuse me . . . Did you have any trouble finding the house?

PUPIL: No . . . Not at all. I just asked the way. Everybody knows you around here.

PROFESSOR: For thirty years I've lived in this town. You've not been here for long? How do you find it?

PUPIL: It's all right. The town is attractive and even agreeable, there's a nice park, a boarding school, a bishop, nice shops and streets . . .

PROFESSOR: That's very true, young lady. And yet, I'd just as soon live somewhere else. In Paris, or at least Bordeaux.

PUPIL: Do you like Bordeaux?

PROFESSOR: I don't know. I've never seen it.

PUPIL: But you know Paris?

PROFESSOR: No, I don't know it either, young lady, but if you'll permit me, can you tell me, Paris is the capital city of . . . miss?

PUPIL: *(Searching her memory for a moment, then, happily guessing)* Paris is the capital city of . . . France?

PROFESSOR: Yes, young lady, bravo, that's very good, that's perfect. My congratulations. You have your French geography at your finger tips. You know your chief cities.

PUPIL: Oh! I don't know them all yet, Professor, it's not quite that easy, I have trouble learning them.

PROFESSOR: Oh! It will come . . . you mustn't give up . . . young lady . . . I beg your pardon . . . have patience . . . little by little . . . You will see, it will come in time . . . What a nice day it is today . . . or rather, not so nice . . . Oh! but then yes it is nice. In short, it's not too bad a day, that's the main thing . . . ahem . . . ahem . . . it's not raining and it's not snowing either.

PUPIL: That would be most unusual, for it's summer now.

PROFESSOR: Excuse me, miss I was just going to say so . . . but as you will learn, one must be ready for anything.

PUPIL: I guess so, Professor.

PROFESSOR: We can't be sure of anything, young lady, in this world.

PUPIL: The snow falls in the winter. Winter is one of the four seasons. The other three are . . . uh . . . spr . . .

PROFESSOR: Yes?

PUPIL: . . . ing, and then summer . . . and . . . uh . . .

PROFESSOR: It begins like "automobile," miss.

PUPIL: Ah, yes, autumn . . .

PROFESSOR: That's right, miss. That's a good answer, that's perfect. I am convinced that you will be a good pupil. You will make real progress. You are intelligent, you seem to me to be well informed, and you've a good memory.

PUPIL: I know my seasons, don't I, Professor?

PROFESSOR: Yes, indeed, miss . . . or almost. But it will come in time. In any case, you're coming along. Soon you'll know all the seasons, even with your eyes closed. Just as I do.

PUPIL: It's hard.

PROFESSOR: Oh, no. All it takes is a little effort, a little good will, miss. You will see. It will come, you may be sure of that.

PUPIL: Oh, I do hope so, Professor. I have a great thirst for knowledge. My parents also want me to get an education. . . .

DICTIONARY WORK

Some of the words and expressions in the scene from *The Lesson* may be unfamiliar or confusing because they have more than one meaning. Here are dictionary-style definitions of some of these words.

When there is more than one meaning, mark the definition that best fits this passage.

agreeable *(adj.)*
1. to one's liking; pleasing
2. suitable; conformable
3. ready to consent or submit

attractive *(adj.)*
1. having the power to draw or pull towards
2. pleasing

bishop *(noun)*   a Christian clergyman of a high rank

to convince *(verb)*
1. to persuade
2. to make somebody feel certain

effort *(noun)*
1. the use of physical or mental energy to do something
2. a difficult exertion of strength or will
3. an earnest attempt
4. something done or produced through exertion; an achievement
5. *(physics)* force applied against inertia

to inform *(verb)*
1. to give information to; make aware of something
2. to acquaint (oneself) with knowledge of a subject

to permit *(verb)*
1. to allow the doing of; consent to
2. to grant consent or leave to; authorize
3. to afford opportunity or possibility for

progress *(noun)*	1. movement, as toward a goal; advancement
	2. development or growth
	3. steady improvement, as of a society or civilization
thirst *(noun)*	1. a sensation of dryness in the mouth and throat related to a need or desire to drink
	2. an insistent desire; a craving

COMPREHENSION QUESTIONS

Answer the following questions based on the scene from the play.

1. Does the professor keep the new pupil waiting?
2. What is the first thing that they do when they meet?
3. How did the pupil find her way to the professor's house?
4. How long have the professor and the pupil lived in the town?
5. The professor says he would prefer to live somewhere else. Where?
6. Does the pupil know the names of many capital cities?
7. When she answers correctly, how does the professor react?
8. When the pupil complains that learning is hard, what does the professor tell her?

POINTS TO CONSIDER AND DISCUSS

1. Why do you think the pupil comes to study with the professor? Give at least two reasons.
2. Why does the professor ask the pupil about Paris? What is he trying to find out?
3. Why does the professor keep changing his mind about the weather?

Word Families

It may help to think about words having "families." Study this chart and note what the words have in common.

NOUN	VERB	ADJECTIVE	ADVERB
agreement	agree	agreeable	agreeably
attraction	attract	attractive	attractively
conviction	convince	convincing	convincingly
information	inform	informative	informatively
permission	permit	permissible	permissibly
progress	progress	progressive	progressively
thirst	thirst	thirsty	thirstily

Using the Vocabulary

Complete the following sentences with words from the chart above or the list of words on pages 6–7. You may have to change the form of the word.

1. The Lewises have been walking for hours, and they're hot, tired, and _____.

2. Please make an _____. You have to try much harder than that.

3. Robin thinks you'll find the new teacher to be an _____ person. She likes her very much.

4. You need a _____ to build a house.

5. We would like to _____ you that you have won the lottery.

6. Since my son started to work harder in school, he has made great _____.

7. If you can _____ me that you really need it, I'll lend you the money.

8. When Minnie smiles, she's really _____. I wonder why she looks so serious most of the time.

Cloze Passage

Choose words from the vocabulary list on pages 6–7 to complete this passage.

THE BISHOP

The (1) _____ is a very (2) _____ man. He makes an (3) _____ to (4) _____ us of the (5) _____ that he makes. He (6) _____ us to ask him questions. Then he tries to (7) _____ us of his ideas.

LANGUAGE

Many students like to learn fixed expressions and use these "chunks of language" in speaking or writing. This kind of learning is very common when you are learning your first language. Ionesco is famous for using fixed expressions in his writing. He does it to show how ordinary people actually speak.

Here is a list of language chunks. Do you understand what they mean?

1. Yes, it's true, believe it or not.

2. When I walked in late, she said, "Better late than never."

3. It's all very well for you to say it's easier said than done. Show me how to do it.

4. I read an article about the picnic in the paper. The reporter said that a good time was had by all.

5. My parents want to choose a husband for me. I said that in this day and age it's just not done.

6. "Go ahead," I said. "Have a ball; don't even think about me."

Read through the following expressions. All of these sentences are taken from the scene you studied.

1. It's hard.

2. I have a great thirst for knowledge.

3. You will make real progress.

4. We can't be sure of anything in this world.

5. I beg your pardon.

6. I'm very sorry to have kept you waiting.

7. How do you find it?

8. It will come . . . have patience.

Choose one of the sentences above to complete these mini-dialogues. Some phrases or sentences may work in more than one mini-dialogue. Try to use all the expressions.

1. a. You are sitting in my seat.

   b. _____

2. a. I didn't know what to expect.

   b. _____

3. a. Is it very easy?

   b. _____

4. a. I'm absolutely sure that I'm right.

   b. _____

5. a. Are you sure that I'll succeed?

   b. _____

6. a. Do you really want to learn?

   b. _____

7. a. I've been here for two hours.

   b. _____

8. a. When will I understand English grammar?

   b. _____

Read these mini-dialogues aloud with a partner. Use contractions and try to sound as natural as possible.

Can you find any other examples of fixed expressions in the text?

WRITING ACTIVITIES*

1. Have you or anyone you know ever had private lessons? What were they for? Describe the lessons. Did the private tutoring help?

2. Describe an ideal learning situation. How many students should there be in a class? How often should the class meet? Describe the best class you ever had.

PROSE PASSAGE

Read this letter from a pupil's mother to a professor:

22 Brown St.
Greenside, CA 99623

October 29, 1998

Dear Professor Black:

My husband and I are very worried about our daughter, June. She is seventeen years old, and we are anxious about her progress at school.

June has problems with geography, and she never picks up a book to read for pleasure. Her teachers also tell us that she has trouble spelling correctly. June is very shy and needs someone to help her to develop self-confidence.

We have heard about you from a number of our friends. They say that you have really helped their children to pass their examinations. Would you be willing to teach June privately? We can pay whatever you normally charge.

Please let us know if you are willing to accept our daughter as your pupil.

Sincerely,

Linda Gray

*A special guide to writing appears at the end of this unit.

Imagine that you are the professor. Write a reply to Ms. Gray.

- Make sure that you refer to all the points she raises in her letter.
- Tell her how much you charge and when you are available to teach her daughter.
- The style of your letter should be formal.
- Don't forget to include your address and the date.

LISTENING TASK

Listen to the dialogue on the tape. As you listen, follow the instructions. Mark the spot on the map to show where the professor lives. Write down his name and address.

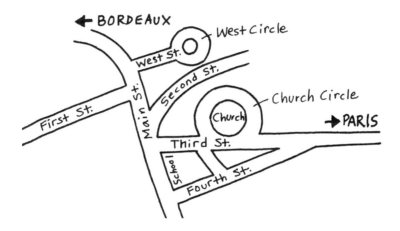

SPECIAL ASSIGNMENTS

1. Do people shake hands when they meet in other countries that you know about? How do they greet each other in different parts of the world? Write your answers in your journal.

2. How do your teachers react when you answer correctly? What happens when your answers are wrong? Answer in your journal.

3. With a friend or classmate, act out the scene from the play. This would be a good scene to learn by heart, as it is filled with useful expressions. Once you feel confident that you know your part, act out the scene. If you have access to the equipment, videotape yourselves or record yourselves on a tape recorder.

4. There is a ballet version of *The Lesson* on videotape. Try to find it through your library. Watch it with your class and then discuss it.

5. If you enjoyed studying the scene from *The Lesson,* try to find another of Ionesco's plays in the library. *The Bald Soprano* is not too difficult for people studying English. The ending of the play is really surprising and shocking.

6. The plays that Ionesco writes come from the *Theater of the Absurd.* Go to the library and see what you can find out about this kind of drama. What more can you find out about Ionesco? Include a picture of Ionesco in your report.

A GUIDE TO WRITING

The following points are first steps to good essay writing. Learn them well, and pay special attention to them while doing the writing activities.

1. Each composition you write should have a title.

2. It should be divided into paragraphs.

3. The beginning of the paragraph must be clearly indicated by indenting the first word several spaces.

4. All sentences must begin with a capital letter and end with a period (full stop), question mark (?), or exclamation mark (!).

5. All proper nouns (names) must begin with a capital letter.

Here are some suggestions for proper paragraphing:

1. A paragraph must contain one topic or main idea. When you finish describing an incident or discussing a point, begin a new paragraph.

2. Each paragraph must have unity. It must be about the same issue, idea, or topic.

Now choose one of the topics under "Writing Activities." After you complete your writing assignment, read it through carefully. Check your spelling, grammar, punctuation, capitals, and paragraphing.

Remember that good writers are never satisfied with the first draft. They write and revise again and again.

UNIT 2   *What Do You Have to Do to Belong?*

INTRODUCTION

Here are some questions for you to think about and discuss:

People who move to another country often have problems trying to fit in. People who move from one city or town to another also have to learn about the new place before they feel that they belong.

What kinds of changes do people need to make to adjust to a new place?

What did you have to do in order to belong to the society in which you now live?

What do other people have to do to be accepted by you and your friends?

Do you think it makes a difference if you were born in the country where you live? Does age make a difference?
Does it make a difference if you are rich or poor?
Educated or not educated?

A B O U T   T H E   P L A Y

Someone who has been through some of these changes is David Henry Hwang. The son of Chinese immigrants, Hwang was born in Los Angeles in 1957. He graduated from Stanford and Yale Universities. Today Hwang is a well-known playwright. His most famous play is *M. Butterfly*, which was also made into a movie.

We are going to study a speech from Hwang's play *FOB*, written in 1978. "FOB" stands for Fresh Off the Boat. The play has three characters. Dale was born in America of Chinese descent; Grace, his cousin, was born in Taiwan but now lives in California; and Steve, Grace's friend, is a newcomer to the U.S. from Hong Kong. In this speech, Grace explains how difficult it was for her to feel that she belonged in the U.S.

This extract is a monologue, a long speech by one person. Remember that Grace's spoken American English is different from the written language. It includes slang and short forms.

David Henry Hwang
from FOB

GRACE: Yeah. It's tough trying to live in Chinatown. But it's tough trying to live in Torrance, too. It's true. I don't like being alone. You know, when Mom could finally bring me to the U.S., I was already ten. But I never studied my English very hard in Taiwan, so I got moved back to the second grade. There were a few Chinese girls in the fourth grade, but they were American-born, so they wouldn't even talk to me. They'd just stay with themselves and compare how much clothes they all had, and make fun of the way we all talked. I figured I had a better chance of getting in with the white kids than with them, so in junior high I started bleaching my hair and hanging out at the beach—you know, Chinese hair looks pretty lousy when you bleach it. After a while, I knew what beach was gonna be good on any given day, and I could tell who was coming just by his van. But the American-born Chinese, it didn't matter to them. They just giggled and went to their own dances. Until my senior year in high school—that's how long it took for me to get over this whole thing. One night I took Dad's car and drove on Hollywood Boulevard, all the way from downtown to Beverly Hills, then back on Sunset. I was looking and listening—all the time with the window down, just so I'd feel like I was part of the city. And that Friday, it was—I guess—I said, "I'm lonely. And I don't like it. I don't like being alone." And that was all. As soon as I said it, I felt all of the breeze—it was really cool on my face—and I heard all of the radio —and the music sounded really good, you know? So I drove home.

DICTIONARY WORK

Some of the words and expressions in the scene from *FOB* may be unfamiliar or confusing because they have more than one meaning. Here are dictionary-style definitions of some of these words.

When there is more than one meaning, mark the definition that best fits this passage.

to bleach *(verb)*	to make or become white by chemical action or sunlight
breeze *(noun)*	a wind, especially a soft and gentle one
to figure *(verb)*	1. to believe, think, conclude, or understand
	2. to appear, have an important part; be prominent
	3. to calculate, compute
to giggle *(verb)*	to laugh in a nervous or silly way
to hang out *(phrasal verb)*	to stay in a particular place
lousy *(adj.)*	1. infested with lice
	2. nasty; bad; ill
tough *(adj.)*	1. *(of meat)* hard to cut
	2. not easily broken or worn out
	3. strong, able to endure hardships
	4. *(of persons)* rough and violent
	5. stubborn, unyielding
	6. hard to carry out, difficult

COMPREHENSION QUESTIONS

Answer the following questions based on the scene from the play.

1. Do you think that Grace's mother wanted to take her to the U.S. before she was ten years old? How do you know? Copy the words from the text that tell you.

2. What do the Chinese American girls talk about?

3. Why does Grace decide to hang out with the white students?

4. What does she do to fit in with them?

5. What happens when Grace takes her father's car for a drive?

POINTS TO CONSIDER AND DISCUSS

1. What do you think Torrance is?

2. Give some examples of why it might be hard to live in Chinatown.

3. Why do you think that Grace says it's tough to live in Torrance?

4. Why do you think she doesn't like to be alone?

5. Grace was put in the second grade in the U.S., even though she had been in a higher grade in her home country. Why? Was that fair? Was it a good idea?

6. Why don't the American-born Chinese girls at her school have anything to do with Grace?

7. How long do you think she continued to bleach her hair?

8. Who do you think that Grace is talking to when she makes this speech?

VOCABULARY

Using the Vocabulary

Complete the following sentences with words from the word list on page 17. You may have to change the form of the word.

1. Sarah still can't _____ that person out. She will never understand her.

2. Because the towel was stained, Mrs. Brown had to _____ it.

3. "Please stop _____ or else I'll have to ask you to leave the room."

4. This place is a _____ for college students. They always come here to meet each other.

5. It's _____ to be an only child. I really wish I came from a big family.

6. It's hot in here. Please open the window so that we can feel the _____.

7. "Do you feel sick? If you feel so _____, maybe you should stay in bed."

Cloze Passage

Use words from the vocabulary list on page 17 to complete this passage.

MY LITTLE SISTER

One day, in order to get in with the white kids, my little sister

(1) _____ her hair. When I saw her, I couldn't

(2) _____ out what she had done. Then I started to

(3) _____. She got angry with me. She said, "I feel so

(4) _____ here in this country. I (5) _____

_____ with my new friends. I try to be like them. It's

(6) _____ when they laugh at me. Please, don't laugh." I

said I was sorry, and I promised not to laugh at her anymore.

LANGUAGE

Contractions

One reason that Grace's speech sounds so natural is that she uses many contractions in her speech. Many students of English as a second or foreign language think that full forms are more correct than contractions. Using full forms makes their speech sound unnatural and bookish.

Here are some of the most common expressions that are usually spoken in a shortened or contracted form:

"TO BE"	POSITIVE	NEGATIVE
I am	I'm	I'm not
you are	you're	you aren't, you're not
he is	he's	he isn't, he's not
she is	she's	she isn't, she's not
it is	it's	it isn't, it's not
we are	we're	we aren't, we're not
they are	they're	they aren't, they're not

(continued)

"TO HAVE" + PAST PARTICIPLE	POSITIVE	NEGATIVE
I have heard	I've heard	I haven't heard
you have heard	you've heard	you haven't heard
he has heard	he's heard	he hasn't heard
she has heard	she's heard	she hasn't heard
it has heard	it's heard	it hasn't heard
we have heard	we've heard	we haven't heard
they have heard	they've heard	they haven't heard

MODALS + VERB	POSITIVE	NEGATIVE
we will see	we'll see	we won't see
Jim will see	Jim'll see	Jim won't see
I would like	I'd like	I wouldn't like

The word "can" is confusing. When you say something like "I can do it," pronounce the word "can" as "cn." The negative form is "can't."

To improve your pronunciation and intonation, read aloud the following sentences from Grace's speech, making sure that you use contractions. Try to record yourself so you can listen to how much more natural you sound when you use contractions.

1. It's tough trying to live in Chinatown.
2. It's true.
3. They wouldn't even talk to me.
4. They'd just stay with themselves and compare their clothes.
5. It didn't matter to them.
6. That's how long it took me to get over this thing.
7. I'd feel like I was part of the city.
8. I'm lonely.
9. I don't like it.
10. I don't like being alone.

Answering Questions

In the following dialogue, a reporter asks Grace some questions. Write suitable answers for her. Use information in Grace's speech to help you with the answers.

Reporter: When did you come to the U.S.?

Grace: _____

Reporter: How old were you?

Grace: _____

Reporter: Did you find it easy to live here?

Grace: _____

Reporter: Did both your parents come to this country?

Grace: _____

Reporter: When you first came here, who were your friends?

Grace: _____

Reporter: How long did it take for you to feel happy here?

Grace: _____

Reporter: Thanks very much. Good luck.

Grace: Goodbye.

Now act out your dialogue with a partner.

Language Chunks

Many students like to learn fixed expressions and use these "chunks of language" in speaking or writing. This kind of learning is very common when you are learning your first language. Grace uses many of these chunks in her speech.

Here is a list of some of these chunks from the scene we studied. Which ones do you think you could use in your own English?

1. It's tough . . .

2. . . . they wouldn't even talk to me.

3. . . . looks pretty lousy . . .

4. I figured I had a better chance . . .

5. . . . to get over this . . .

WRITING ACTIVITIES

1. What kinds of things do people find different when they move to a new country? Make a list.

2. If you have moved to a new country or town, what was easy or difficult for you? Explain.

3. Write a letter to friends or relatives in another country to warn them about problems that they might have when they move to a new country. What advice would you give them?

PROSE PASSAGE

Here is a letter that Grace wrote to some relatives who still live in Taiwan.

> 2120 Bello Ave., Torrance, CA 90802
>
> April 16, 1997
>
> Dear Uncles, Aunts, and Cousins,
>
> I guess you're surprised to get a letter from me after all these years. I got your address from my Mom who says she's sorry she hasn't kept in touch with you. I hope you still live in the same place so this letter will reach you.
>
> Do you remember me? I was only ten when we left Taiwan, but I remember you all. I have happy memories of the great times we spent together as a family.
>
> Our life here is very different from the old country. I had some trouble getting to know America and learning to hang out with the crowd. Once I even bleached my hair!
>
> If you answer this letter, I'll know that you want to keep in touch so I'll write more next time.
>
> 'Bye for now.
>
> Love,
>
> Grace

After reading this letter, answer it as if you were one of the members of the family. You can be either an uncle, aunt, or cousin. Make sure that what you write looks like a letter.

LISTENING TASK

Listen to the listening task recorded on the tape. Write down the information.

SPECIAL ASSIGNMENTS

1. Practice reading Grace's speech aloud. Then ask a friend or classmate to listen to it. Ask for suggestions about how you could improve your reading. If you have access to a tape recorder, record your reading. Maybe your teacher will have time to listen to it and to make comments. Offer to critique a friend's reading. What can you suggest to help him or her?

2. Prepare a two-minute talk to give to your class on the topic "What it means to be American [or any other nationality you can speak about]."

3. Go to your library to find out more information about David Henry Hwang. Share the information you find with your class.

4. Draw a picture of what you think Grace looks like.

5. Can you write a song for Grace? If you can, write both the music and the words. Otherwise, you can write new words to a tune you already know.

6. Using a tape recorder, interview a new immigrant about his or her experiences after arriving in the country. Transcribe the interview and then edit it. Write a short newspaper article based on the information in the interview.

7. If you could meet Grace today, what kind of person do you think she would be? Describe Grace, mentioning what kind of job you imagine she has, where she lives, whether she is married or single, and what kinds of clothes she wears.

UNIT 3 *You Are What You Eat*

INTRODUCTION

Here are some questions for you to think about and discuss:

What do you think that the title of this unit means?

Do you agree with this idea?

Do you worry about the kind of food that you eat?

Why do some people worry more than others?

Do you think that educated people worry more than
uneducated people?

What effect does sugar have on your health?

Should pregnant women be more careful about their diet than
people who are not pregnant?

What sorts of foods can have a bad effect on unborn babies?

What do you think is a healthy diet?

What kinds of foods do you like to eat?

Do you think that people who move to a new
country should change their diet?

A B O U T   T H E   P L A Y

Eating properly during pregnancy is a major concern in this scene from *The Baby Dance* by Jane Anderson. Anderson is an American playwright. *The Baby Dance* was first performed at the Pasadena Playhouse, California, in 1992.

The play is about a couple who cannot have children. They arrange to adopt a child from a poor couple who already have four children. The following dialogue is between Wanda, the pregnant mother, and Rachel, the woman who wants to adopt her baby. In this scene, Rachel is trying to give Wanda advice about her diet. Notice that the two women are using informal spoken American English.

Jane Anderson
from THE BABY DANCE

***Don't forget to read the stage directions as
well as the dialogue.***

WANDA: . . . Do you want dessert?

RACHEL: Sure.

WANDA: I made some Jello with topping. I thought it'd keep us cool.

RACHEL: Do you have any fruit?

WANDA: I got some peaches. Would you like that?

RACHEL: I love peaches. That would be perfect.

WANDA: *(Gets out a container of canned peaches)* They're kinda warm. I
could stick them in the freezer to cool them up for you.

RACHEL: You know what? You don't have to do that. I'll have the Jello.

WANDA: Are you sure? It's no trouble.

RACHEL: No, the Jello would be perfect.

WANDA: I think you'll like it better. It's more refreshing.

> *(Wanda sets two cups of bright red Jello on the table and spoons
> some Cool Whip on top of each.)*

> *(They both taste their Jello dessert.)*

RACHEL: Oh, this is very good.

WANDA: It's the red raspberry. It's one of their better flavors.

RACHEL: My mother used to make me Jello.

WANDA: Oh really?

RACHEL: Oh, sure. When I was sick. Jello is very comforting.

WANDA: I give my kids Jello all the time. It's good for them. It's supposed
to make their nails strong.

RACHEL: Oh, it does. You know, sometimes I buy the plain gelatin base
without the sugar. Knox makes it.

WANDA: Yeah but the kids won't take it like that. They want something
that tastes good.

RACHEL: Well, if you mix it with a little fruit juice . . .

WANDA: Honey, it don't matter. No matter what you give 'em, kids only
want to eat certain things. The only thing Kevin will eat is Sloppy

Joe mix. Doesn't matter what else you put in front of him, if it isn't Sloppy Joe mix, he won't eat it.

RACHEL: Did you breast feed . . . ?

WANDA: I breast fed some. But bottles are more convenient.

RACHEL: That's what my mother always said. But they're finding out that a lot of these formulas have sugar in them.

WANDA: Well, the formula I've used has always worked. None of my babies had any problems. They gained twice their weight in the first six months.

RACHEL: Uh-huh.

WANDA: You're gonna have to use formula.

RACHEL: My doctor recommended a special brand.

WANDA: The name brands are just as good.

RACHEL: Well, my doctor says this one is very good.

WANDA: Do you know anyone else who's used this formula?

RACHEL: No. Most of my friends breast feed.

WANDA: Uh-huh. Well my advice is to stick to the name brands. They've been around for years and you know they work. That's what I would use.

RACHEL: Well, let me think about it.

WANDA: You want some coffee or anything?

RACHEL: Do you have decaf?

WANDA: I could go next door. I think one of my neighbors has some Sanka.

RACHEL: No, that's fine.

WANDA: I'm gonna re-heat a little for myself. The baby makes me sleepy this time of day.

RACHEL: Wanda . . . *(She stops herself.)* Uh, did you talk to Dr. Costales about drinking coffee?

WANDA: Yes.

RACHEL: What did he say?

WANDA: He said I could have it in moderation.

RACHEL: He said you could have regular coffee? Not decaf?

WANDA: Yuh.

DICTIONARY WORK

Some of the words and expressions in the scene from *The Baby Dance* may be unfamiliar or confusing because they have more than one meaning. Here are dictionary-style definitions of some of these words.

When there is more than one meaning, mark the definition that best fits this passage.

brand *(noun)*	1. trademark or trade name; particular kind of goods with such a mark
	2. piece of burning wood (in a fire)
	3. iron used red-hot, for burning a mark into a surface
comfort *(noun)*	1. state of being free from suffering, anxiety, or pain
	2. help or kindness to a person who is suffering
	3. person or thing that brings relief or help
convenient *(adj.)*	easy to use; handy
dessert *(noun)*	course of fruit or sweets served at the end of a meal
formula *(noun)*	1. set form of words used regularly
	2. statement of a rule or principle in mathematics
	3. set of directions, usually in symbols, as for a medical preparation
	4. milk mixture for a baby
to gain *(verb)*	1. to get more of something, as power or possessions; to acquire wealth
	2. to increase in weight
moderate *(adj.)*	keeping or kept within reasonable limits
plain *(adj.)*	1. easy to see, hear, or understand
	2. simple, ordinary; without luxury or ornament

to recommend *(verb)*	1. to speak favorably of; say that one thinks something is good
	2. to suggest as wise or suitable
refreshing *(adj.)*	1. strengthening; giving rest and relief
	2. welcome and interesting because rare and unexpected
regular *(adj.)*	1. evenly arranged; symmetrical; systematic
	2. taking place at fixed intervals
	3. properly qualified or trained
	4. belonging to a full-time or standing army
	5. according to correct procedure or behavior
	6. ordinary, normal; customary

COMPREHENSION QUESTIONS

Answer the following questions based on the scene from the play.

1. Can you describe the weather in this scene? How do you know what it is like?

2. Why does Wanda say that the Jello is more refreshing than the peaches?

3. In what way is Jello supposed to be healthy?

4. Why does Rachel recommend the plain gelatin base?

5. What kind of food do Wanda's children like?

6. How do most of Rachel's friends feed their babies?

7. Why will Rachel have to use formula?

POINTS TO CONSIDER AND DISCUSS

1. Describe the relationship between the two women. Why are they so polite to each other?

2. Which woman is more concerned about health? Explain.

3. Examine the language the women use. Who has more education? How do you know?

4. Why do you think that Rachel refuses to eat the Jello at first?

5. What is wrong with the peaches that Wanda offers Rachel?

6. Is there a special reason that Rachel tells Wanda that her mother used to make her Jello?

7. Which is better for babies: formula or breast milk? Can you explain why?

8. What's the difference between regular and decaffeinated coffee?

9. Why does Rachel ask Wanda whether she talked about coffee with her doctor?

10. Is Rachel surprised to hear Wanda's reply? Do you think her doctor really agreed that Wanda could drink regular coffee?

VOCABULARY

Word Families

It may help to think about words having "families." Study this chart and note what the words have in common.

NOUN	VERB	ADJECTIVE	ADVERB
comfort	comfort	comfortable comforting	comfortably comfortingly
convenience		convenient	conveniently
moderation	moderate	moderate	moderately
		plain	plainly
recommendation	recommend	recommendable recommended	recommendably
refreshment	refresh	refreshing	refreshingly
regularity	regulate regularize	regular	regularly

Using the Vocabulary

Complete the following sentences with words from the chart on page 30 or the word list on pages 28–29. You may have to change the form of the word.

1. Annie: Would you like something sweet after your dinner?

    Perhaps a _____? I _____ the chocolate

    cake. It's delicious, but I can't eat any. I need to go on a diet. I've

    been _____ too much weight.

    Betty: Thanks, I'd love some cake. This is an excellent

    _____ of coffee. Where did you buy it?

2. My meaning is quite _____. You can't have it.

3. Don't overdo anything. Try to be _____ at all times.

4. Issy has no _____ work. Perhaps that's why he's

    homeless.

5. Ruth is quite _____, thanks. She doesn't need anything.

6. The house is near schools and bus routes. It's really very

    _____.

7. Dr. Robinson feels much better now. She had such a

    _____ sleep.

Cloze Passage

Complete this story with words from the word list on pages 28–29.

GOING SHOPPING

I went to the supermarket to do some shopping. My husband

(1) _____ that I buy (2) _____ coffee. He

says that the Star (3) _____ is the most

(4) _____. I prefer (5) _____ decaf. So I

bought two kinds of coffee.

Then I looked for a (6) _____. I wanted something

that would be (7) _____, as I am too lazy to cook.

I suppose that's the reason that I bought ice cream for my husband.

I try to be (8) _____ because I don't want to

(9) _____ weight, so I bought fruit for myself. In the

end, I bought two kinds of coffee and two kinds of dessert.

LANGUAGE

In the scene you read, there are many contractions and other casual forms typical of spoken American English style. Can you recognize the difference between formal written English and informal spoken English? Here is a list of sentences in English. Mark each one F for formal written English or I for informal spoken English.

1. I got up and left. Then I turned and thanked him for his time.
2. Which freeway? Did you say San Diego?
3. Go and take a look, if you can spare the time.
4. You happen to notice that they're not there anymore?
5. When he picked up the phone, I knew he was ready to end our conversation.
6. Rodriguez is supposed to be doing some work for me, but he didn't show up.
7. I got nothing to do with him, okay?
8. You gonna say they're wrong?
9. Been a long time since I slept good.
10. A few trees and shrubs grew near the house.
11. Go help those poor little kids.

Change the following sentences to a more formal written style. The first sentence has been done as an example. All the sentences are taken from the scene in the play.

1. I got some peaches. *(I have some peaches.)*
2. It's supposed to make their nails strong.
3. Yeah but the kids won't take it like that.
4. Honey, it don't matter.
5. Doesn't matter what else you put in front of him, if it isn't Sloppy Joe mix, he won't eat it.
6. You're gonna have to use formula.
7. They've been around for years and you know they work.

WRITING ACTIVITIES

1. Write a letter to someone you know well who does not eat the right kinds of food. What advice would you give the person to make sure that he or she eats a healthy diet?
2. Write a dialogue between two people who are having a meal together. Try to use some of the polite expressions you read in this play.
3. Write a recipe for a cake or another special dish from the country where you were born.

PROSE PASSAGE

Rachel wants Wanda to eat. On the next page you'll find the recipe for Rachel's favorite salad.

TASTY TUNA SALAD

Ingredients

1 large tomato	2 tablespoons lowfat mayonnaise
2 cloves garlic	salt and pepper
1 6½-ounce can water-packed tuna	lettuce leaves
	sprigs of parsley

Instructions for using the ingredients are given out of order. Rearrange the steps so that they make sense. The first instruction is correct. (Hint: Recipes list ingredients in the order that they are used.)

Method

1. Chop the tomato into small pieces.
2. Add the garlic to the chopped tomato.
3. Decorate with parsley and serve cold.
4. Add the mayonnaise and salt and pepper to taste.
5. Mix gently and pile on top of the lettuce leaves.
6. Flake the tuna and add it to the mixture.
7. Peel the garlic and crush it or chop it up.

LISTENING TASK

Listen to this lecture on diet. The lecturer will name ten foods that are very healthy and good for you. As you listen, read the list of foods in this exercise. Which foods does the lecturer mention?

1. pasta
2. crackers
3. broccoli
4. garlic
5. apples
6. cantaloupe
7. bagels
8. orange juice
9. Jello
10. whole-wheat bread
11. Sloppy Joe mix
12. cheese
13. lowfat yogurt
14. peas
15. tofu
16. pancakes
17. tomatoes
18. dried beans
19. watercress
20. peaches

SPECIAL ASSIGNMENTS

1. Working with a partner, act out the scene from the play. Try to make your accent as American as possible. If possible, videotape or record your performance and then play it back. What can you do to improve your reading?

2. Make a list of all the food that you eat for a week. Compare your list with a classmate's. Who eats a healthier diet?

3. Explain how your diet changed when you moved from one country to another. What did you eat in your old country? What do you eat now? Which kind of food do you prefer?

4. Find a recipe in a cookbook or magazine that you would like to prepare. Try it out and describe what happened. How did you feel about the whole process?

UNIT 4   Are We Ready for the Future?

INTRODUCTION

Here are some questions for you to think about and discuss:

> The world has changed a lot since our grandparents were born. What do you think are the most important changes that have happened?
>
> In what ways will our grandchildren's lives be different from ours?
>
> Make a list of things you use once and then throw away. How would these lists differ around the world? Give examples.
>
> Many people don't seem to worry about saving our planet. They are not careful of the way they use resources such as electricity, water, wood, and paper. How do you feel about this?

A B O U T   T H E   P L A Y

I n her play *Mud,* Maria Irene Fornes gives us some ideas of how she thinks the world will change. Fornes was born in Cuba in 1930 and came to the United States in 1945. Like Ionesco, she has been influenced by the Theater of the Absurd. *Mud* was first performed in 1983. In 1996, it was produced on Broadway in New York. The playwright has received many awards, such as the Obie for Sustained Achievement in the Theater in 1982.

This scene has two characters. Mae is a young woman in her mid-twenties. She is a believer and a very serious person. Henry is a man in his mid-fifties. Although he can hardly read, he likes to think about life a lot. Note that for spoken English, the language used here is rather formal.

María Irene Fornes
from MUD

Don't forget to read the stage directions as well as the dialogue.

HENRY: Soon everything will be used only once. We will use things once. We will need to do that as our time will be of value and it will not be feasible to spend it caring for things: washing them, mending them, repairing them. We will use a car till it breaks down. Then, we will discard it. A radio or any machine or appliance will be discarded as soon as it breaks down. We will make a call on the telephone and a new one will be delivered. Already we see places that use paper cups, paper plates, paper towels.—Our time will not be wasted and we will choose how to spend it.

MAE: I don't think I'll be wanted in such a world.

HENRY: Why not?

MAE: Oh. *(Pause.)* In such a world a person must be of value.

HENRY: Oh?

MAE: I feel I am hollow . . . and offensive. *(As Mae places the dishes on the mantelpiece.)*

HENRY: Why is that?

MAE: I think most people are.

HENRY: What do you mean?—Explain what you mean.

MAE: I don't think I can.

HENRY: I am not offensive. I don't think I am offensive. I think I am a decent man.

MAE: You are decent, Henry. I know you are. . . .

HENRY: Then, what do you mean when you say we are offensive?

MAE: I mean that we are base, and that we spend our lives with small things.

HENRY: I don't feel I do that.

MAE: Don't be offended, Henry. You are not base.

Some of the words and expressions in the scene from *Mud* may be unfamiliar or confusing because they have more than one meaning. Here are dictionary-style definitions of some of these words.

When there is more than one meaning, mark the definition that best fits this passage.

appliance *(noun)*
an electrical device or instrument designed to perform a specific household function, such as a toaster or dishwasher

base *(adj.)*
1. having a mean-spirited or selfish lack of human decency
2. lacking high values or ethics
3. inferior in value or quality

to break down *(phrasal verb)*
1. to cause to collapse; destroy
2. to become or cause to become distressed or upset
3. to have a physical or mental collapse

decent *(adj.)*
1. acting within recognized standards of propriety or morality
2. free from indelicacy; modest

to discard *(verb)*
to throw away; reject

feasible *(adj.)*
1. capable of being done or brought about; possible
2. capable of being used or dealt with successfully; suitable
3. logical; likely

hollow *(adj.)*
1. having a cavity, gap, or space within
2. deeply indented or concave; sunken
3. without substance or character
4. lacking truth or validity

to mend *(verb)*
1. to make repairs or restoration to; fix
2. to reform or correct

to offend *(verb)*	1. to cause displeasure, anger, resentment, or hurt feelings
	2. to be displeasing or disagreeable
to repair *(verb)*	1. to restore to sound condition after damage or injury; fix
	2. to set right; remedy
	3. to go to a specific location
value *(noun)*	an amount, as of goods, services, or money, considered to be a fair and suitable equivalent for something else; a fair price or return

COMPREHENSION QUESTIONS

Answer the following questions based on the scene from the play.

1. Why does Henry think that in the future we will only use things once?

2. What examples does Henry give of things that we will discard in the future?

3. What kinds of things do we already only use once, according to Henry?

4. When things break down, how will we get new ones?

5. Does Mae feel that most people are just like her? Why?

6. Does Mae include Henry when she talks about other people?

POINTS TO CONSIDER AND DISCUSS

1. Why does Mae feel that she won't be wanted in a world like the one Henry mentions?

2. How does Mae think that people will spend their time? Do you agree with her?

3. Are Mae and Henry optimistic or pessimistic about the future? How do you feel about the future?

4. What do you think Henry means by the statement "Our time will be of value"? What will people do with their time?

Word Families

It may help to think about words having "families." Study this chart and note what the words have in common.

NOUN	VERB	ADJECTIVE	ADVERB
baseness	abase	base	basely
decency		decent	decently
discard	discard	discarded discardable	
feasibility		feasible	feasibly
hollow	hollow	hollow	hollowly
mend	mend	mended mendable	
offense	offend	offensive	offensively
repair	repair	repaired repairable	
value	value	valuable	

Using the Vocabulary

Complete the following sentences with words from the chart above or the word list on pages 38–39. You may have to change the form of the word.

1. I'm sorry if I _____ you. I don't mean to do that.

2. Yes, that's a _____ way to solve the problem. I think it'll work.

3. What is the _____ of that diamond? It looks very expensive.

4. Don't worry. We can easily _____ the hole in your sock.

5. The Gonzalez family bought a new _____ for their kitchen.

6. Gregory is a _____ man. I respect and trust him.

7. When an appliance _____ _____, my wife

can usually _____ it herself.

8. That statue is so light because it's _____.

Adjectives

Adjectives are used with nouns to describe them or to add information about them. They usually come before the noun, but may come after if connected to the noun by a linking verb:

- We sat on the **hollow** log.

- That log is **hollow.**

Some of the adjectives used in this scene may be new to you. Learning new adjectives is a good way to improve your writing and speech.

Match the following adjectives in column A to a suitable noun in column B. Some adjectives may match more than one noun.

A	B
valuable	promise
hollow	comment
offensive	painting
decent	suggestion
base	person
feasible	act

Complete the following sentences with a compatible adjective and noun. The first one has been completed for you.

1. Although he said he would help me, I didn't believe him. I knew it

was a _____*hollow*_____ _____*promise*_____.

2. The thief stole a _____ _____ from the

museum.

3. An insult or something unpleasant that you say about another person is an _____ _____.

4. Someone who is ready to help others and who can be trusted is a _____ _____.

5. A crime of violence is a _____ _____.

6. A _____ _____ is one that is logical and can be used.

Make up sentences of your own using the adjectives in column A.

Pronunciation

In the scene from the play, there are many sentences written in the future tense. When we want to talk about something in the future that we think will happen, we use *will* + the base form of the verb. *Will* can be contracted to *'ll*. In the negative form, we use *will not* and *won't*.

Here are some examples:

1. She thinks she'll pass the test.
2. I'll rent another house next year.
3. Do you think it'll be sunny and hot tomorrow?
4. They won't be able to finish their homework before they go to the movies.
5. We don't think they'll go without us.
6. I'll make sure that he does it; don't worry.
7. She must work harder or she won't pass this test.

Find all the sentences in the scene from the play that are written in the future tense. Copy five examples and change them to the contracted form. The first one has been done for you.

We will use a car till it breaks down.

We'll use a car till it breaks down.

Choose the best answer. The first one has been done for you.

1. Your friend Dina is planning to buy a new bicycle soon. What does she tell you?

   a. I buy a new bike next week.
   (b.) I'll buy a new bike next week.

2. She wants you to go with her to give her some advice. What does she say to you?

   a. Do you go with me to buy the bike?
   b. Will you go with me to buy the bike?

3. You agree to go with her. What do you say?

   a. OK, I'll go with you.
   b. OK, I come with you.

4. You want to know where the money will come from. What do you ask her?

   a. Where will you get the money?
   b. Where do you get the money?

5. You see a bike that Dina likes. You ask her what she plans to do. She says:

   a. I take it.
   b. I'll take it.

6. You ask Dina if her parents will let her ride the bike to school. She says:

   a. I won't be able to. It's too far.
   b. I'm not able to. It's too far.

WRITING ACTIVITIES

1. Read the dialogue again and then write your own conclusion to it.
2. How do you as a private citizen try to take care of the earth? Make a list.

PROSE PASSAGE

Many books have been written about the future. One of the most famous is *Future Shock* by Alvin Toffler, written in 1970. This is what Toffler thinks will happen to the family in the future.

In the future, there will be fewer people in the family. In the old days, families had many children. Families were made up of parents, grandparents, children, uncles and aunts, and cousins. This kind of family was very good because people took care of each other.

Today, this kind of family does not work so well. It is difficult and expensive to move a large family. In order to get a job today, workers must be ready to move to places where jobs can be found. In the Western world today, most families are small. They are made up of parents and very few children.

In the future, it may be better for couples to delay having a family while they are working. So a typical family of the future will be only a husband and wife. According to Margaret Mead, the famous anthropologist, some families will be "chosen" to have children. Others will work and not have any children. Many families will wait until they retire from their jobs before they have children. New developments in science will make it possible for people to have children when they are old.

Here are three sentences that were left out of the passage you just read. Place them in the text where they belong.

1. It was not unusual to have ten or more children in a family.

2. Workers may have to move many times during their lives.

3. In the future, people will probably live much longer lives.

LISTENING TASK

Listen to this speech given by Ngan Pham. While you listen, read the text of Ngan's talk. Try to fill in the missing words.

Hi, I'm Ngan Pham from the O. B. Whaley Elementary School in

San Jose, California. I'm ten years old and I'll be talking to you

(1) _____ teachers of the twenty-first century. Being a

teacher in the twenty-first century will (2) _____ a lot
different from now. It (3) _____ be easier for teachers
and students.

The classroom will (4) _____ because everyone will
get a computer. The computer hard drive will have
(5) _____ work instead of (6) _____ it into
your desk. The computer will also have your books. If you
(7) _____ read, the computer will read to you
(8) _____ you can follow along and learn to read.

(9) _____ will be in the computer, including your ref-
erence books, text books, math books, and (10) _____
books. With the computer you will not have a messy
(11) _____ to clean up. Learning will be easier for students (12) _____ of (13) _____ thinking cap.
The thinking cap has a computer chip inside to help students remember (14) _____ they are reading about.

Teachers in the twenty-first century will (15) _____
need a lot (16) _____ training. They will go to school
and learn things to teach (17) _____ students. They will
learn many things (18) _____ we do. Teachers will need
lots of training on computers because they have to plan
(19) _____ for the students. The teachers will also have
to set up (20) _____ programs for the students so that
the students will be (21) _____ to read along
(22) _____ the computer.

Many times students get sick and can't come to school.
(23) _____ in the future, when students get sick and

can't (24) _____ to school, they'll take their computers home and the computers will show (25) _____ what the teacher said. If there is (26) _____, the teacher will fax it to them.

In conclusion, (27) _____ think that teaching will be easier (28) _____ the best job in the twenty-first century.

SPECIAL ASSIGNMENTS

1. Read the scene aloud a few times with a partner. Try to help your partner with his or her pronunciation. Ask your partner to make suggestions about your pronunciation. When you are satisfied with your reading, try to record yourselves.

2. Make up an advertisement to try to get people to buy a new appliance. It could be for newspaper, television, or radio. Explain all the advantages of the product. If you like drawing, illustrate your advertisement.

3. Imagine that you are an anthropologist like Margaret Mead. Write down your vision of what the world will be like in the future. Refer to the Prose Passage for some ideas.

4. Describe the kind of world you think your grandchildren will live in.

5. Who should take care of whom in a family? Refer to the Prose Passage for some ideas. Should both parents work?

6. In the Prose Passage there is a statement: "New developments in science will make it possible to have children when you are old." Has this prediction come true? Find articles in newspapers, magazines, or on the Internet about this subject. What do you think about children who have parents who are much older?

UNIT 5   *What Is This All About?*

INTRODUCTION

Here are some questions for you to think about and discuss:

> Some people believe that a person's childhood can lead them to a life of crime. What do you think?
>
> Do you think that people who are not criminals can be influenced to break the law?
>
> Have you ever heard of people who change, for example, in wartime? Explain.

A B O U T   T H E   P L A Y

The criminal way of life is on view in this scene from *The Dumb Waiter*, by the British playwright Harold Pinter. Like Ionesco's, Pinter's plays come from the Theater of the Absurd. This play was first performed in London in 1960.

The language of Pinter's plays is simple, but the ideas are very complex. The person reading the play or watching it in the theater has to work hard to understand what is happening. Critics have said that Pinter writes beautifully and passionately. His work is funny and very frightening at the same time. His style is original, but it captures the sound of real spoken English. Very few other playwrights can do this as well as Pinter can.

In this scene, you'll hear the voices of Gus and Ben, two gunmen who have been hired to kill somebody. They are waiting in an old house for their orders. They use very simple English, but there is something strange about the way they speak. Many people think that Ben is a threatening person, someone they would be afraid to meet.

Harold Pinter
from THE DUMB WAITER

Don't forget to read the stage directions as well as the dialogue.

GUS: Ben, look here.
BEN: What?
GUS: Look.

(Ben turns his head and sees the envelope. He stands.)

BEN: What's that?
GUS: I don't know.
BEN: Where did it come from?
GUS: Under the door.
BEN: Well, what is it?
GUS: I don't know.

(They stare at it.)

BEN: Pick it up.
GUS: What do you mean?
BEN: Pick it up!

(Gus slowly moves towards it, bends and picks it up.)

What is it?
GUS: An envelope.
BEN: Is there anything on it?
GUS: No.

BEN: Is it sealed?

GUS: Yes.

BEN: Open it.

GUS: What?

BEN: Open it!

(Gus opens it and looks inside.)

What's in it?

(Gus empties twelve matches into his hand.)

GUS: Matches.

BEN: Matches?

GUS: Yes.

BEN: Show it to me.

(Gus passes the envelope. Ben examines it.)

Nothing on it. Not a word.

GUS: That's funny, isn't it?

BEN: It came under the door?

GUS: Must have done.

BEN: Well, go on.

GUS: Go on where?

BEN: Open the door and see if you can catch anyone outside.

GUS: Who, me?

BEN: Go on!

(Gus stares at him, puts the matches in his pocket, goes to his bed and brings a revolver from under the pillow. He goes to the door, opens it, looks out and shuts it.)

GUS: No one.

(He replaces the revolver.)

BEN: What did you see?

GUS: Nothing.

BEN: They must have been pretty quick.

(Gus takes the matches from pocket and looks at them.)

GUS: Well, they'll come in handy.

BEN: Yes.

GUS: Won't they?

BEN: Yes, you're always running out, aren't you?

GUS: All the time.

BEN: Well, they'll come in handy then.

GUS: Yes.

BEN: Won't they?

GUS: Yes, I could do with them. I could do with them too.

BEN: You could, eh?

GUS: Yes.

BEN: Why?

GUS: We haven't got any.

BEN: Well, you've got some now, haven't you?

GUS: I can light the kettle now.

BEN: Yes, you're always cadging matches. How many have you got there?

GUS: About a dozen.

BEN: Well, don't lose them. Red too. You don't even need a box.

> *(Gus probes his ear with a match.)*

> *(Slapping his hand)* DON'T WASTE THEM! GO ON, GO AND LIGHT IT.

GUS: Eh?

BEN: Go and light it.

GUS: Light what?

BEN: The kettle.

GUS: You mean the gas.

BEN: Who does?

GUS: You do.

BEN: *(His eyes narrowing)* What do you mean, I mean the gas?

GUS: Well, that's what you mean, don't you? The gas.

BEN: *(Powerfully)* If I say go and light the kettle I mean go and light the kettle.

GUS: How can you light a kettle?

BEN: It's a figure of speech! Light the kettle. It's a figure of speech!

GUS: I've never heard it.

BEN: Light the kettle! It's common usage!

GUS: I think you've got it wrong.

BEN: *(Menacing)* What do you mean?

GUS: They say put on the kettle.

BEN: *(Taut)* Who says?

(They stare at each other, breathing hard.)

(Deliberately) I have never in all my life heard anyone say put on the kettle.

GUS: I bet my mother used to say it.

BEN: Your mother? When did you last see your mother?

GUS: I don't know, about—

BEN: Well, what are you talking about your mother for?

(They stare.)

Gus, I'm not trying to be unreasonable. I'm just trying to point out something to you.

GUS: Yes, but—

BEN: Who's the senior partner here, me or you?

GUS: You.

BEN: I'm only looking after your interests, Gus. You've got to learn, mate.

GUS: Yes, but I've never heard—

BEN: *(Vehemently)* Nobody says light the gas! What does the gas light?

GUS: What does the gas—?

BEN: *(Grabbing him with two hands by the throat, at arm's length)*
THE KETTLE, YOU FOOL!

(Gus takes the hands from his throat.)

GUS: All right, all right.

(Pause)

BEN: Well, what are you waiting for?

GUS: I want to see if they light.

BEN: What?

GUS: The matches.

(He takes out the flattened box and tries to strike.)

No.

(He throws the box under the bed.)
(Ben stares at him.)

DICTIONARY WORK

Some of the words and expressions in the scene from *The Dumb Waiter* may be unfamiliar or confusing because they have more than one meaning. Here are dictionary-style definitions of some of these words.

When there is more than one meaning, mark the definition that best fits this passage.

to come in handy *(phrasal verb)* — to be useful

dozen *(noun)* — a set of twelve

figure of speech — striking or effective expression, usually made by comparing or identifying one thing with another

kettle *(noun)*
1. a metal pot, usually with a lid, for boiling or stewing
2. a teakettle

mate *(noun)*
1. one of a matched pair
2. a spouse
3. either of a breeding pair of animals or birds
4. a good friend or companion; an associate

partner *(noun)*
1. one of a pair or team in a sport, game, or activity, such as tennis, bridge, or dancing
2. a spouse
3. a member of a business partnership

reasonable *(adj.)*
1. capable of reasoning; rational
2. governed by or in accordance with reason or sound thinking
3. within the bounds of common sense
4. not excessive or extreme; fair

revolver *(noun)* — a pistol having a revolving cylinder with several cartridge chambers that may be fired in succession

to run out	1. to get used up; become exhausted
(phrasal verb)	2. to put out by force; compel to leave
	3. to become void, especially through the passage of time or an omission
seal *(noun)*	1. a substance used to close or secure something or to prevent seepage of moisture or air
	2. a marine mammal with webbed flippers
senior *(noun)*	1. a person who is older than another; a senior citizen
	2. someone of higher position, rank, or grade than another in the same set or class
	3. a student in the final year of high school or college

COMPREHENSION QUESTIONS

Answer the following questions based on the scene from the play.

1. What did someone put under the door?
2. What is in the envelope?
3. Is there anything written on the envelope?
4. Was there anyone outside?
5. What does Gus do with the matches?
6. What does he take out that was under the pillow?
7. Do they need the matches?
8. What do they plan to do with them?
9. What do Ben and Gus argue about with regard to boiling water?
10. Can Gus actually light something with the matches?

1. Do you think that Gus and Ben trust each other? Explain.
2. Do you think that they understand the world that they live in?
3. What kind of education do you think Ben and Gus had?
4. The two men seem to be bored and irritable. Why do you think this is so?
5. Why do they argue about language? Who wins the argument?
6. Some critics say that Ben and Gus are like people in the lower ranks of the army. What do you think?
7. Who is the senior partner?
8. What kind of movie does this scene remind you of?

VOCABULARY

Complete the following sentences with words from the word list on pages 54–55. You may have to change the form of the word.

1. Kevin, while you're at the supermarket, please buy a

   _____ eggs. And buy some extra milk in case we

   _____ _____.

2. Joanna promises you'll have the papers tomorrow: signed,

   _____, and delivered.

3. Ms. Miller, the secretary, can't make important decisions without

   asking the _____ _____ first.

4. Take a needle and thread with you on your trip, Richard. I'm sure

   they'll _____ _____ _____ if

   you need to sew something.

5. I'm trying to be _____. I can't help it if Alice is being

   completely unreasonable.

6. Last week Sandra bought an electric _____ for her mother's birthday. Mrs. Baker loves to drink tea.

7. In this state you need a license to buy a _____ or any other kind of gun.

8. In Australia, it's quite common to hear a man call his friend "_____."

Here are some more useful words from the text. Complete these sentences with one of these words.

catch	anyone
pillow	towards
menacing	match
stared	replace
examine	power

1. "Come on baby, light my fire," said the kettle to the _____.

2. He didn't _____ the ball, so they lost the game.

3. Terrorism is threatening and _____.

4. "Let me _____ your ear," said the flea to the dog.

5. Will _____ be at home tomorrow afternoon? The electrician is coming to _____ the switch.

6. I jumped off the tracks because the train was coming _____ me.

7. After they broke up, Dan cried into his _____ at night.

8. My enemy came near, but I didn't run away. I just _____ fiercely at him.

When Ben talks about lighting the kettle, he is using a figure of speech called *metonymy*. Metonymy is the use of the name of one thing for that of another to which it has some logical relation.

In the following sentences, at least one word is substituted for another that it symbolizes. Find each metonymy and explain the sentences. Are there examples of metonymy in your first language? Compare them to the English examples.

1. Yes, he's drunk, I'm afraid. He's much too fond of the bottle.
2. Some people believe that the government should take care of them from the cradle to the grave.
3. The judge told the prisoner to have respect for the bench.
4. The palace should not look down on the cottage.
5. "Two men look out through the same bars; / One sees the mud, and one the stars."
6. Brenda: Life's really tough!

   Bill: I never promised you a rose garden.
7. I thought life would be a bowl of cherries. I'm afraid it isn't.

Language Chunks

Many students like to learn fixed expressions and use these "chunks of language" in speaking or writing. This kind of learning is very common when you are learning your first language.

Here is a list of some of these language chunks from the scene we studied. Do you understand what they mean?

1. Look here.
2. What's that?
3. Where did it come from?
4. What is it?
5. I don't know.
6. Who, me?

7. Pick it up.

8. That's funny, isn't it?

9. Go on.

10. They'll come in handy.

Choose one of these sentences to reply in the following mini-dialogues. Some phrases or sentences may work in more than one mini-dialogue. Try to use a different expression for each reply.

1. a. Do we need those pencils?

   b. _____

2. a. Pick it up!

   b. _____

3. a. What do you think about it?

   b. _____

4. a. I'm afraid to do it.

   b. _____

5. a. I have something for you.

   b. _____

6. a. I just got a new book in the mail.

   b. _____

7. a. Who wants to speak to me?

   b. _____

8. a. You dropped the letter.

   b. _____

Read these mini-dialogues aloud with a partner. Use contractions and try to sound as natural as possible. Can you find any other examples of fixed expressions in the text?

1. Go back to the scene and try to write more dialogue for Gus and Ben. What do you think happens next in the scene?

2. In your journal, write about your reactions to this scene by Harold Pinter. Is it easy to understand? Do you understand why Harold Pinter is so famous?

3. Write a letter to Ben and Gus in prison. Give them advice on what they should or should not do when they are released.

PROSE PASSAGE

At the beginning of plays, the playwright usually sets the scene through detailed stage directions. Read the opening stage directions Harold Pinter wrote for *The Dumb Waiter*.

Scene: A basement room. Two beds, flat against the back wall. A serving hatch, closed, between the beds. A door to the kitchen and lavatory, left. A door to the passage, right.

Ben is lying on a bed, left, reading a newspaper. Gus is sitting on a bed, right, tying his shoelaces, with difficulty. Both are dressed in shirts, trousers, and braces.

Silence.

Gus ties his laces, rises, yawns, and begins to walk slowly to the door, left. He stops, looks down, and shakes his foot.

Ben lowers his paper and watches him. Gus kneels and unties his shoelace and slowly takes off his shoe. He looks inside it and brings out a flattened matchbox. He shakes it and examines it. Their eyes meet. Ben rattles his paper and reads. Gus puts the matchbox in his pocket and bends down to put on his shoe. He ties his lace, with difficulty. Ben lowers his paper and watches him. Gus walks to the door, left, stops, and shakes the other foot. He kneels, unties his shoelace, and slowly takes off the shoe. He looks inside it and brings out a flattened cigarette packet. He shakes it and examines it. Their eyes meet. Ben rattles his paper and reads. Gus puts the packet in his pocket, bends down, puts on his shoe and ties the lace.

He wanders off, left.

Ben slams the paper down on the bed and glares after him. He picks up the paper and lies on his back, reading.

Silence.

A lavatory chain is pulled twice off, left, but the lavatory does not flush.

Silence.

Gus re-enters, left, and halts at the door, scratching his head.

Ben slams down the paper.

Imagine that you are directing the play.

1. Tell either Gus or Ben what you want them to do. Make a list of instructions for how to move and how to act.

2. Draw a picture of the stage. Place the furniture. Where are the doors? Show the position of the serving hatch. Add any other details that you think are important.

LISTENING TASK

Listen to this talk about Harold Pinter's childhood. Then read through the list of statements. Mark the statements T (true) or F (false). If they are false, correct them.

1. Harold Pinter was born in London, England.
2. He was born on October 30, 1910.
3. His family came from Europe to live in England.
4. His mother was a tailor.
5. The family lived in a working-class area.
6. Mrs. Pinter was a marvelous cook.
7. Mr. Pinter worked terribly hard.

8. During the war, Harold Pinter stayed home.

9. When he had to leave the house, he took his cricket bat with him.

10. In 1944, he saw a flying bomb.

11. Hackney Downs Grammar School accepts boys and girls.

12. Pinter loved all his teachers.

13. His favorite teacher was Joseph Brearly.

14. Mr. Brearly taught Latin.

15. Pinter acted in *Macbeth* and *Romeo and Juliet*.

16. Mr. Brearly directed Pinter in two plays.

17. He never played any sport at school.

18. He never wanted to study at Cambridge and Oxford.

19. Harold Pinter was a Latin scholar.

20. Harold Pinter studied at a university.

SPECIAL ASSIGNMENTS

1. Read the dialogue aloud with a partner. This scene really works well if you act it out. Try to find a toy gun, matches, and an envelope to use as props. As the sentences are very short, it would be good to learn the lines by heart. Don't worry if it's not exactly as Pinter wrote it; just have fun.

2. Ask the librarian or your teacher for a copy of the entire play *The Dumb Waiter*. Try to see a production of the play, or find out if there is a movie version available. If you enjoy this, try reading some other Pinter plays, such as *The Caretaker* or *The Birthday Party*. Harold Pinter also writes many film scripts. Try to find and watch some of his films.

3. Try to describe the two men in *The Dumb Waiter*. Mention their ages, height, weight, and any scars they may have. Do they have beards or mustaches? Use your imagination. If the police asked you for a description of these men, could you give an accurate picture of them? If you are artistic, draw pictures of Ben and Gus.

4. Find out what you can about Harold Pinter in the library. Try to find a picture of him. Some critics say that Pinter achieves his effect of terror because the terror is nameless. Can you explain this? Read what critics say about Harold Pinter. You might ask the librarian to help you. Report on your research to the class.

UNIT 6   Fathers and Daughters

INTRODUCTION

Here are some questions for you to think about and discuss:

The way that families treat each other is changing in many parts of the world. Many parents try to be more of a friend to their children than before.

How do you think parents or caregivers should talk to their children?

If and when you have children, will you speak to them the same way you were spoken to?

Is there any difference in the way mothers and fathers talk to their children?

What kind of topics do you discuss with your parents or children?

Why is it important for families to talk to each other?

Do you agree that there has been a change in the way family members treat each other?

ABOUT THE PLAY

In this scene from the 1991 play *Tender Offer* by Wendy Wasserstein, we will study how a father and his daughter talk to each other. Wasserstein was born in New York in 1950. She won a Pulitzer Prize and a Tony Award for her most famous play, *The Heidi Chronicles* (1988). In all her plays, Wasserstein uses humor to share serious ideas with the audience.

You'll hear the voices of Paul, the father, and Lisa, the daughter, in this scene. Pay attention to the differences between the English spoken here and the style of written English.

Wendy Wasserstein
from TENDER OFFER

LISA: Daddy, what do you think about? I mean, like when you're quiet what do you think about?

PAUL: Oh, business usually. If I think I made a mistake or if I think I'm doing okay. Sometimes I think about what I'll be doing five years from now and if it's what I hoped it would be five years ago. Sometimes I think about what your life will be like, if Mount Saint Helens will erupt again. What you'll become if you'll study penmanship or word processing. If you speak kindly of me to your psychiatrist when you are in graduate school. And how the hell I'll pay for your graduate school. And sometimes I try and think what it was I thought about when I was your age.

LISA: Do you ever look out your window at the clouds and try to see which kinds of shapes they are? Like one time, honest, I saw the head of Walter Cronkite in a flower vase. Really! Like look don't those kinda look like if you turn it upside down, two big elbows or two elephant trunks dancing?

PAUL: Actually still looks like Walter Cronkite in a flower vase to me. But look up a little. See the one that's still moving? That sorta looks like a whale on a thimble.

LISA: Where?

PAUL: Look up. To your right.

LISA: I don't see it. Where?

PAUL: The other way.

LISA: Oh, yeah! There's the head and there's the stomach.

DICTIONARY WORK

Some of the words and expressions in the scene from *Tender Offer* may be unfamiliar or confusing because they have more than one meaning. Here are dictionary-style definitions of some of these words.

When there is more than one meaning, mark the definition that best fits this passage.

actually *(adv.)*
1. existing and not merely potential or possible
2. at the present moment; current
3. based on fact

business *(noun)*
1. a person's occupation, work, or trade
2. commercial, industrial, or professional dealings
3. serious work or endeavor
4. an affair or matter

to erupt *(verb)*
1. to emerge violently from restraint or limits; explode
2. to become violently active
3. to force out or release something, such as steam, with violence or suddenness

graduate *(noun)*
one who has received an academic degree or diploma

kind *(adj.)*
1. of a friendly, generous, or warm-hearted nature
2. showing sympathy or understanding; charitable
3. humane; considerate

penmanship *(noun)*
the art, skill, style, or manner of hand-writing

psychiatrist *(noun)*
a medical doctor who specializes in mental or emotional problems

stomach *(noun)*	the abdomen or belly
thimble *(noun)*	a small cup made of metal or other hard material, worn for protection on the finger that pushes the needle in sewing
whale *(noun)*	a very large marine mammal
word processing *(noun)*	the creation, editing, and production of documents and texts by means of computer systems

COMPREHENSION QUESTIONS

Answer the following questions based on the scene from the play.

1. What does the father often think about?
2. What does Paul worry about in connection with Lisa's schooling?
3. Does Paul ask Lisa what she thinks about? Explain.
4. What kind of pictures does Lisa see in the clouds? What kind of pictures does Paul see?
5. Do they ever see the same picture? Explain.

POINTS TO CONSIDER AND DISCUSS

1. How old do you think Lisa and her father are?
2. Where do you think they are when they have this talk?
3. Are the things that Paul thinks about typical of fathers you know?
4. Does Paul think that Lisa will have problems and will have to see a psychiatrist one day? Explain.
5. How do we know that Paul really tries to understand his daughter?

VOCABULARY

Complete the following sentences with words from the word list on pages 67–68. You may have to change the form of the word.

1. When volcanoes _____, there is usually a lot of damage to property.

2. In the Bible there is a famous story about a _____ who swallowed Jonah.

3. You say you are telling me the truth, but I _____ don't believe one word you say.

4. Which do you put first in your life, your family or your _____?

5. If Ken doesn't work much harder, he won't _____ at the end of the year.

6. If Martha would wear a _____ when she sews, she wouldn't hurt her finger.

7. Mom, I can't go to school today because I have a _____ ache.

8. Why does Steve need a new computer? He only uses it for _____ _____.

9. Helen is so sad and unhappy. She's been depressed for weeks. Do you think she should see a _____?

10. Most of my Vietnamese students have beautiful _____. Do they learn it in school?

This play takes place in the United States. In spoken American English, phrases such as "going to," "want to," "have to," "has to," "kind of," and "sort of" are reduced and changed to one word as shown below:

going to → gonna
want to → wanna
have to → hafta
has to → hasta
kind of → kinda
sort of → sorta

In this play, Wasserstein actually writes "kind of" and "sort of" as "kinda" and "sorta." This is not common practice. However, if you want to sound like an American, it's a good idea to speak this way.

Read the following sentences with an American accent. Use the reduced form of the underlined phrases.

1. I have to know by next week.
2. I want to try that again.
3. We're going to see that show next month.
4. It's kind of slow, don't you think?
5. It has to be now or never.
6. He's sort of handsome, I think.
7. Who's going to give me the money?
8. When do you want to leave?
9. That's a waste of time.
10. Please give me some of that.
11. It really looks out of date.
12. You have plenty of time.

1. Write a dialogue between a parent and child. If you can, try to recreate a discussion between you and your parent or caregiver.

2. Look out the window at the clouds. Do any of them look like something else? Describe what you see.

3. Write a letter to an older person you respect. Ask for advice about your future or your child's future.

PROSE PASSAGE

Here is a letter written by a teenager to Dear Abby, a famous newspaper advice columnist. The teenager has several problems and needs help solving them.

After reading this letter, write your own letter to Abby asking for help or advice.

Dear Abby,

I recently overheard some kids at school talking about me. They called me "funny face." I'm sure that's the reason why I don't have many friends and I hardly ever get invited to parties.

But my worst problems are at home. My father is only interested in his business. When he does spend time with me, he never shows any interest in what I think or feel about things.

My mother yells, "Do this" and "Don't do that." She complains about me all the time. It's always "You're always late!" or "You're so messy and untidy!"

I've had enough! I can't go on like this! Can you help me?

Yours,

Sandy Redman

Listen to this lecture about Deborah Tannen's work. Professor Tannen is an expert on the differences between the language of men and women. This lecture is about differences between boys and girls. While you listen, mark the following statements T (true) or F (false) according to what the professor says.

1. Boys and girls speak the same way.
2. Men and women don't use language the same way.
3. Boys usually play with boys, and girls play with girls.
4. Girls usually play outside.
5. Boys like to tell jokes and stories.
6. Boys' games never have winners and losers.
7. Jump rope and hopscotch are girls' games.
8. A girl's best friend is very important to her.
9. Girls say, "Get outta here!"
10. Boys say, "Gimme that!"
11. Girls want other girls to like them.
12. Boys want to win and be the best.

SPECIAL ASSIGNMENTS

1. Read the dialogue aloud with a partner. Try to sound as American as possible. Practice the scene a few times and then perform it for your class and your teacher.
2. Try to imagine what Paul and Lisa look like. Describe them to a partner or a small group. What kind of business does Paul work in? What does Lisa like to do for fun? What do you think she's going to be when she grows up?
3. Go to the library and find out as much as you can about Wendy Wasserstein. Write a short biography of her.

4. Tell what you know about word processing. Do you know how to use a computer? What do you use it for?

5. After listening to the lecture by Professor Tannen, describe the differences between boys and girls in the culture you know best. Use the statements in the Listening Task to help you with your composition.

UNIT 7   *Will You Marry Me?*

INTRODUCTION

Here are some questions for you to think about and discuss:

Many parents find it difficult to accept that their children are old enough to start dating. It can be even harder when the child is interested in someone of a different family background or religion.

Do you think that parents should allow teenagers to go out with anyone they choose?

At what age should young people start dating?

Can young people choose their partners in other countries? Give examples.

Do young people start dating at the same age around the world?

Do you know anyone who married someone from another culture? Describe the differences in their backgrounds.

Explain how the marriage worked out.

A B O U T   T H E   P L A Y

In her play *A Taste of Honey*, Shelagh Delaney describes a relationship between a white, working-class, teenage woman and a black sailor. The play takes place in Salford, Lancashire, which is in England. The time is the present.

Born in 1939, Shelagh Delaney wrote this play when she was eighteen years old. It was first produced at the Theatre Royal in London in 1958. The play won two national awards and was later made into a film. Delaney still lives in Salford, England. It is interesting to note that she left school at the age of sixteen.

Shelagh Delaney
from A TASTE OF HONEY

Don't forget to read the stage directions as well as the dialogue.

(Jo and her boyfriend, a colored naval rating,* walking on the street. They stop by the door.)

JO: I'd better go in now. Thanks for carrying my books.

BOY: Were you surprised to see me waiting outside school?

JO: Not really.

BOY: Glad I came?

JO: You know I am.

BOY: So am I.

JO: Well, I'd better go in.

BOY: Not yet! Stay a bit longer.

JO: All right! Doesn't it go dark early? I like winter. I like it better than all the other seasons.

BOY: I like it too. When it goes dark early it gives me more time for— *(He kisses her.)*

JO: Don't do that. You're always doing it.

BOY: You like it.

JO: I know, but I don't want to do it all the time.

BOY: Afraid someone'll see us?

JO: I don't care.

BOY: Say that again.

JO: I don't care.

BOY: You mean it too. You're the first girl I've met who really didn't care. Listen, I'm going to ask you something. I'm a man of few words. Will you marry me?

JO: Well, I'm a girl of few words. I won't marry you but you've talked me into it.

BOY: How old are you?

**naval rating:* sailor

JO: Nearly eighteen.

BOY: And you really will marry me?

JO: I said so, didn't I? You shouldn't have asked me if you were only kidding me up. *(She starts to go.)*

BOY: Hey! I wasn't kidding. I thought you were. Do you really mean it? You will marry me?

JO: I love you.

BOY: How do you know?

JO: I don't know why I love you but I do.

BOY: I adore you. *(Swinging her through the air)*

JO: So do I. I can't resist myself.

BOY: I've got something for you.

JO: What is it? A ring!

BOY: This morning in the shop I couldn't remember what sort of hands you had, long hands, small hands or what. I stood there like a damn fool trying to remember what they felt like. *(He puts the ring on and kisses her hand.)* What will your mother say?

JO: She'll probably laugh.

BOY: Doesn't she care who her daughter marries?

JO: She's not marrying you, I am. It's got nothing to do with her.

BOY: She hasn't seen me.

JO: And when she does?

BOY: She'll see a colored boy.

JO: No, whatever else she might be, she isn't prejudiced against color. You're not worried about it, are you?

BOY: So long as you like it.

JO: You know I do.

BOY: Well, that's all that matters.

JO: When shall we get married?

BOY: My next leave? It's a long time, six months.

JO: It'll give us a chance to save a bit of money.

Some of the words and expressions in the scene from *A Taste of Honey* may be unfamiliar or confusing because they have more than one meaning. Here are dictionary-style definitions of some of these words.

When there is more than one meaning, mark the definition that best fits this passage.

to adore *(verb)*
1. to worship as God or a god
2. to regard with deep, often rapturous love
3. to like very much

colored *(adj.)*
1. of or belonging to a racial group not regarded as white
2. of mixed racial strains
3. appear different from reality

to kid *(verb)*
1. to mock playfully; tease
2. to deceive in fun; fool

leave *(noun)*
1. permission to do something
2. official permission to be absent from work or especially military duty
3. the period of time granted by such permission
4. an act of departing; a farewell

prejudice *(noun)*
1. the holding of unreasonable preconceived judgments or convictions
2. irrational suspicion or hatred of a particular group, race, or religion

probably *(adv.)*   most likely; presumably

to resist *(verb)*
1. to strive to fend off or offset an action, effect, or force
2. to remain firm against such actions; withstand
3. to keep from giving in to or enjoying something

COMPREHENSION QUESTIONS

Answer the following questions based on the scene from the play.

1. Where was Jo?
2. Who was waiting for her?
3. What did the boy carry for her?
4. Was Jo glad to see him?
5. Which is Jo's favorite season?
6. Why does the boyfriend like this season?
7. Does Jo mind if people see them kissing?
8. How old is Jo?
9. Do Jo and the boy love each other?
10. How will Jo's mother feel about this marriage?
11. When do they plan to marry?
12. What do they plan to do to prepare for the marriage?

POINTS TO CONSIDER AND DISCUSS

1. Jo's boyfriend carries her books for her. Do boys carry their girl-friend's books in all countries?
2. What does "a man of few words" mean?
3. Jo says: "I won't marry you but you've talked me into it." What does she mean? Is she joking when she says "no"?
4. Do you believe Jo when she says that her mother is not preju-diced? Is this common?
5. Do you think that Jo is too young to be married? Explain.

VOCABULARY

Complete the following sentences with words from the word list on page 78. You may have to change the form of the word.

1. Some people are _____ against people of other

   religions.

2. You're _____ me. You're pulling my leg. I don't believe you.

3. The new grandparents simply _____ their grandchild.

4. When I'm on a diet, I still can't _____ eating chocolate.

5. Jimmy's late. He's _____ stuck in traffic.

6. Helen's husband is coming home on _____ from the navy for two weeks. She's very excited.

LANGUAGE

Asking Questions

One of the problems that many students have in speaking English is asking good questions. If you examine the scene you read, you will notice that most of the dialogue is made up of questions and answers. Read the following answers from the scene. Look at the question that was asked. Write the original question. Then make up another question. The first one has been completed as an example.

1. Not really. *(Were you surprised to see me waiting outside school?)*
   Do you know how to speak Greek?

2. You know I am. _____

   _____

3. I don't care. _____

   _____

4. I won't marry you. _____

   _____

5. Nearly eighteen. _____

   _____

6. I don't know why I love you but I do. _____

_____

7. She'll probably laugh. _____

_____

8. It's got nothing to do with her. _____

_____

9. So long as you like it. _____

_____

10. It's a long time, six months. _____

_____

Language Chunks

Many students like to learn fixed expressions and use these "chunks of language" in speaking or writing. This kind of learning is very common when you are learning your first language. Jo and her boyfriend use many of these chunks in their speech.

Here is a list of some of these chunks from the scene we studied. Do you understand the meaning of these expressions? Which ones do you think you could use in your own English?

1. I'd better go in now.
2. Thanks for carrying my books.
3. Not really.
4. You know I am.
5. So am I.
6. Not yet.
7. Don't do that.
8. I don't care.
9. Say that again.
10. I said so, didn't I?

Use the expressions above to reply to the following statements. The first one is done for you.

1. a. I'm really hungry.

   b. <u>So am I.</u>

2. a. Do you really forgive me?

   b. _____

3. a. Are you ready to go home?

   b. _____

4. a. Can I have the last piece?

   b. _____

5. a. Didn't you hear me?

   b. _____

6. a. Are you ready for the test?

   b. _____

Read these mini-dialogues aloud with a partner. Use contractions and try to sound as natural as possible.

WRITING ACTIVITIES
....

1. Write a letter to your parents to tell them about someone you met whom you think you may marry.
2. Write the next part of the scene. Try to copy Shelagh Delaney's style.

PROSE PASSAGE
....

If you want to look for the man or woman of your dreams, you may decide to join a dating service to help you to find him or her. Here is a form from a dating service. Fill it out for fun.

THE VALENTINE DATING CLUB

Information about You

Name: _____

Address: _____

Phone number: _____ E-mail address: _____

❑ Male   ❑ Female   Age: _____   Height: _____   Weight: _____

Race: _____   National origin: _____

Religion: _____   Primary language: _____

Highest level of education: _____

Occupation: _____   Annual income: _____

I am now   ❑ single   ❑ married   ❑ divorced   ❑ widowed

❑ I have   ❑ I have not   had children

❑ I would   ❑ I would not   like to have children in the future

My primary objective is   ❑ to meet friends   ❑ to date a lot

❑ a steady relationship   ❑ marriage

My work schedule is: _____

My favorite hobbies and leisure activities are: _____

Information about the Person You Would Like to Meet

I would like to meet a   ❑ male   ❑ female   Age range: _____

How do you want to be contacted?

❑ E-mail only   ❑ Phone only   ❑ Both e-mail and phone

How will you submit payment?

❑ Credit card   Number: _____ Expiration date: _____

❑ Check or money order; please make payable to Valentine Dating Service

The sailor in *A Taste of Honey* is ready to be married. There is another sailor in the poem "Seaman's Ditty," by Gary Snyder, who was not ready to marry when he was young. Read the poem and try to fill in the missing words. Note that some of the missing words rhyme with other words in the poem. Other missing words are repeated in the poem. Then listen to a reading of the poem and check whether the words you wrote are the correct ones.

SEAMAN'S DITTY
Gary Snyder

I'm wondering where you are now

Married or mad or free;

Wherever you are you're likely glad,

But memory troubles (1) _____.

We could've had us children

We could have had a (2) _____

But you thought not, and I (3) _____ not,

And these nine years we roam.

Today I worked in the deep dark tanks,

And climbed out to watch the (4) _____;

Gulls and salty waves pass by,

And mountains of Araby.

I've traveled the lonely oceans

And wandered the (5) _____ towns.

I've learned a (6) _____ and lost a lot,

And proved the world was (7) _____.

Now if we'd stayed together,

There's much we'd never've known—

But dreary books and (8) _____ lands

Weigh on (9) _____ like a (10) _____.

SPECIAL ASSIGNMENTS

1. Record the scene with a classmate. Try to sound as if you're speaking English rather than reading it. Listen to the recording. How well did you succeed?

2. Find out what you can about Shelagh Delaney in your library. Write a biography of this playwright.

3. Role-play a scene between a parent and a child who is dating someone that the parent does not like.

4. Watch the movie version of *A Taste of Honey*. Report on it to the class.

5. How do young people behave on a date in your culture? Describe a typical date.

6. Do you believe that you should only marry a person from a similar background? Explain your reasons.

UNIT 8 *Will You Help Me Find a Job?*

INTRODUCTION

Here are some questions for you to think about and discuss:

Have you ever asked anyone to help you to find a job?

Do you know anyone who found a job with the help of someone else? Can you explain what happened?

If you needed to find a job, how would you go about looking for one?

Do you think it's a good idea to work for someone you know?

Would you ask a friend or family member to help you to find a job?

A B O U T   T H E   P L A Y

In this scene from *A Doll's House* by Henrik Ibsen, Nora Helmer asks her husband to give her friend, Mrs. Linde, a job. Although Nora and Torvald Helmer have been married for eight years, they don't really know each other. Nora knows, however, that to get her husband to do something for her, she has to flatter and praise him. Many people think that this play was one of the first works of literature to make us think seriously about the role of women in society. Because it was written over a hundred years ago (in 1879), the language used is rather formal. Remember also that this play was translated from Norwegian.

Ibsen, like Ionesco, is usually referred to by his family name. He was born in Norway in 1828 and died in 1906. His plays have been translated into many languages and are still produced all over the world.

In this scene, you'll hear the voices of three people. Torvald Helmer is going to be a manager of a bank. His wife, Nora, is a housewife. She sounds rather childish in this scene, but it is an act put on for her husband. Nora's friend, Christine Linde, has come to pay a surprise visit to Nora. They have not seen each other for many years.

Henrik Ibsen
from A DOLL'S HOUSE

Don't forget to read the stage directions as well as the dialogue.

NORA: May I introduce you—? This is Christine. She's just arrived in town.

HELMER: Christine—? Forgive me, but I don't think—

NORA: Mrs. Linde, Torvald dear. Christine Linde.

HELMER: Ah. A childhood friend of my wife's, I presume?

MRS. LINDE: Yes, we knew each other in earlier days.

NORA: And imagine, now she's traveled all this way to talk to you.

HELMER: Oh?

MRS. LINDE: Well, I didn't really—

NORA: You see, Christine's frightfully good at office work, and she's mad to come under some really clever man who can teach her even more than she knows already—

HELMER: Very sensible, madam.

NORA: So when she heard you'd become head of the bank—it was in her local paper—she came here as quickly as she could and—Torvald, you will, won't you? Do a little something to help Christine? For my sake?

HELMER: Well, that shouldn't be impossible. You are a widow, I take it, Mrs. Linde?

MRS. LINDE: Yes.

HELMER: And you have experience of office work?

MRS. LINDE: Yes, quite a bit.

HELMER: Well then, it's quite likely I may be able to find some job for you—

NORA: *(Claps her hands)* You see, you see!

HELMER: You've come at a lucky moment, Mrs. Linde.

MRS. LINDE: Oh, how can I ever thank you—?

HELMER: There's absolutely no need.

DICTIONARY WORK

Some of the words and expressions in the scene from *A Doll's House* may be unfamiliar or confusing because they have more than one meaning. Here are dictionary-style definitions of some of these words.

When there is more than one meaning, mark the definition that best fits this passage.

absolute *(adj.)*
1. perfect in quality or nature; complete
2. not mixed; pure
3. not limited by restrictions or exceptions; unconditional
4. unqualified in extent or degree; total
5. not to be doubted or questioned; positive

childhood *(noun)*
time during which one is a child

experience *(noun)*
1. knowledge gained by trial and practice
2. skill and wisdom gained by actually doing things
3. the actual living through of events and emotions

to imagine *(verb)*
1. to form a mental picture or image of something
2. to think

mad *(adj.)*
1. angry; resentful
2. suffering from a disorder of the mind; insane

	3. lacking restraint or reason; foolish
	4. feeling or showing strong liking or enthusiasm
to presume *(verb)*	1. to take for granted as being true
	2. to give reasonable evidence for assuming; appear to prove
	3. to venture without authority or permission; dare
sensible *(adj.)*	1. perceptible by the senses or by the mind
	2. readily perceived; appreciable
	3. having the faculty of sensation; able to feel or perceive
	4. acting with or showing good sense
widow *(noun)*	a woman who has not married again after her husband's death

COMPREHENSION QUESTIONS

Answer the following questions based on the scene from the play.

1. Does Nora use her friend's first or family name to introduce her to her husband?
2. When were Nora and Christine friends?
3. What is Torvald Helmer's new position?
4. How could people find out about Helmer's new position?
5. Does Mrs. Linde have experience working in an office?

POINTS TO CONSIDER AND DISCUSS

1. Do you think Helmer has ever heard of Mrs. Linde? Explain.
2. Why does Helmer presume that Christine is Nora's childhood friend?
3. Has Mrs. Linde really come to town to ask Helmer for a job?
4. Who is "the clever man" that Nora refers to? Why does she say this?

5. Why does Mrs. Linde need to find a job?

6. Do you think that Helmer will give her a job in the bank?

7. Why does Nora ask her husband to help her friend find a job?

VOCABULARY

Complete the following sentences with words from the word list on pages 89–90. You may have to change the form of the word.

1. After Sandra's husband died, her family told her that the

   _____ thing for a _____ to do was to find

   another husband.

2. When Tom was young, he had some bad _____. That's

   the reason he doesn't like to talk about his _____.

3. "I _____ that you have _____ no idea who

   took the money out of mother's purse," he said sarcastically.

4. When Joseph acts strangely, don't _____ that he's

   _____. Actually, he's just angry.

LANGUAGE

When you are having a conversation with someone and you want the person to agree with what you just said, it is common to use a tag question. For example, Nora says, "Torvald, you will, won't you?" to try to persuade her husband.

Answer the following tag questions. The first one is done for you.

1. You do like me, don't you?

   Of course I do.

2. Sheila did finish her homework, didn't she?

   _____

3. My uncle will pay for us, won't he?

_____

4. James is coming, isn't he?

_____

5. Steve dances beautifully, doesn't he?

_____

6. The Johnsons are coming for dinner, aren't they?

_____

7. You will lend me the money, won't you?

_____

8. I am going to the party, aren't I?

_____

9. You have got the money, haven't you?

_____

10. I was going to speak to him about it, wasn't I?

_____

WRITING ACTIVITIES

1. Write a letter to someone in your family or a close friend to ask for help in getting a job.
2. Write a dialogue between a person who is applying for a job and the interviewer.
3. In your journal, describe the kind of job you'd really like to have.

PROSE PASSAGE

Complete this job application.

NAVALLE PUBLISHERS INC. An Equal-Opportunity Employer

Application for Employment

All qualified applicants will receive equal opportunity for employment without regard to race, creed, color, national origin, sex, or age.

NAME _____
        LAST   FIRST   MIDDLE

ADDRESS _____

_____
        CITY   STATE   ZIP CODE

TELEPHONE _____ SOCIAL SECURITY NUMBER _____

| DO NOT WRITE HERE—OFFICE USE ONLY | TO BE COMPLETED IF AND WHEN EMPLOYED |

DATE OF INTERVIEW _____ POSITION _____

SALARY _____ INTERVIEWED BY _____

HIRE _____ DEPARTMENT _____

SPECIAL NOTES _____

_____

DATE OF BIRTH _____ MARITAL STATUS _____

MAIDEN NAME IF APPLICABLE _____

EMPLOYMENT DATA

REFERRED BY _____ SALARY DESIRED _____

POSITION DESIRED ❏ FULL-TIME ❏ PART-TIME ❏ SUMMER ❏ TEMPORARY ❏ OTHER

Are you ready to work overtime as required? ❏ YES ❏ NO

PERSONAL DATA

If you are not a U.S. citizen, what is your Alien Registration or Visa Classification Form number? _____

Have you ever been convicted of any violation of law other than a minor traffic violation?
❏ YES   ❏ NO

If yes, indicate disposition. _____

MEDICAL HISTORY

Do you have any medical problem that would prevent you from performing the job you applied for?   ❏ YES   ❏ NO

If yes, please explain:

_____

_____

(continued)

EDUCATION

	NAME AND ADDRESS	MAJOR	DID YOU GRADUATE?	DATES OF ATTENDANCE
High School				
College or University				
Postgraduate				
Other				

PREVIOUS EMPLOYMENT

Are you employed now? _____ If so, may we contact your present employer? _____

Present or last employer _____

Address _____

Telephone _____

Position/title _____ Immediate supervisor _____

From: Month _____ Year _____ Starting salary $ _____ per _____

To: Month _____ Year _____ Final salary $ _____ per _____

Reason for leaving _____

Describe major duties _____

_____

Signature of Applicant _____ Date _____

LISTENING TASK

Listen to this talk about how to interview for a job. Mark the statements that the speaker actually makes.

Do's and Don'ts for a Job Interview

1. Come at least a half hour to one hour early.
2. Make sure that you arrive on time.
3. Do dress smartly but simply.
4. Wear your most elegant, best clothes.
5. Do bring all your diplomas and/or certificates showing qualifications.

6. You don't need to bring diplomas or certificates; you can send them later.

7. If they ask for references, you can send them later.

8. Do bring references showing previous experience.

9. Try to be courteous and cheerful.

10. Be your own natural self. Don't be too formal.

11. Don't talk too much or too loudly.

12. Make sure that you talk a lot. Silence is suspicious.

13. Your qualifications and experience will tell the employers all they need to know.

14. Don't "oversell" yourself; your qualifications and experience should speak for themselves.

15. Don't criticize the work conditions or the salary.

16. Be sure that you tell them what you really think about the conditions and salary.

Can you add any other Do's and Don'ts?

SPECIAL ASSIGNMENTS

1. This scene from *A Doll's House* has three people. Form groups of four students. One will be the director and the other three will act the scene. It is not a long scene, so it would be best to learn your part by heart. Act the scene and listen to any suggestions made by the director to improve it. Help each other with pronunciation. When you are pleased with your acting, perform the scene for your teacher and class.

2. There are a number of movie versions of this play. Ask your teacher to show the movie to the class. If you enjoy this, try to read the whole play.

3. Find out what you can about Henrik Ibsen in your library. Write a short biography of his life. Can you find a picture of him?

4. What is the best way to find someone really good to employ? What would you do?

UNIT 9 Nature or Nurture?

Here are some questions for you to think about and discuss:

> What makes you the kind of person you are? Some people think that the main influence comes from your genes: you are the way you are because of your ancestors. This is what is meant by "nature." On the other hand, many people think that what you are comes from "nurture." What they mean is that the place where you grew up, your schooling, and all the experiences that you go through make you into the kind of person you are. Most people seem to think that it's a mixture of both that makes you into the kind of person you are.

> What do you think about the influence of nature and nurture on people?

> Before you read the scene from the play, tell a classmate or a group about someone you know or have heard about who got into trouble with the law. Do you think it was nature or nurture that made that person go wrong?

A B O U T   T H E   P L A Y

Characters struggle to understand where a child went wrong in this scene from *'night, Mother* by Marsha Norman. Born in 1947, Norman won a Pulitzer Prize for her play. In this scene, a mother and her daughter, Jessie, are discussing Jessie's son Ricky. Jessie seems to believe that Ricky's problems can mostly be blamed on what he inherited from her and her ex-husband. Her mother doesn't agree.

The play takes place in the U.S. and is set in the present. There are only two characters: Mama and Jessie. Cecil is Jessie's ex-husband and Ricky's father. Neither Ricky nor Cecil appears on stage.

In this scene from the play, you will hear the voices of Mama and Jessie. Remember that this is spoken English. There are different rules for the use of spoken and written English, and you should pay attention to the differences.

Marsha Norman
from 'NIGHT, MOTHER

Don't forget to read the stage directions as well as the dialogue.

MAMA: Ricky will grow out of this and be a real fine boy, Jess. But I have to tell you, I wouldn't want Ricky to know we had a gun in the house.

JESSIE: Here it is. I found it.

MAMA: It's just something Ricky's going through. Maybe he's in with some bad people. He just needs some time, sugar. He'll get back in school or get a job or one day you'll get a call and he'll say he's sorry for all the trouble he's caused and invite you out for supper someplace dress-up.

JESSIE: *(Coming back down the steps)* Don't worry. It's not for him, it's for me.

MAMA: I didn't think you would shoot your own boy, Jessie. I know you've felt like it, well, we've all felt like shooting somebody, but we don't do it. I just don't think we need . . .

JESSIE: *(Interrupting)* Your hands aren't washed. Do you want a manicure or not?

MAMA: Yes, I do, but . . .

JESSIE: *(Crossing to the chair)* Then wash your hands and don't talk to me any more about Ricky. Those two rings he took were the last valuable things I had, so now he's started in on other people, door to door. I hope they put him away sometime. I'd turn him in myself if I knew where he was.

MAMA: You don't mean that.

JESSIE: Every word. Wash your hands and that's the last time I'm telling you. . . .

MAMA: Ricky is too much like Cecil.

JESSIE: He is not. Ricky is as much like me as it's possible for any human to be. We even wear the same size pants. These are his, I think.

MAMA: That's just the same size. That's not you're the same person.

JESSIE: I see it on his face. I hear it when he talks. We look out at the world and we see the same thing: Not Fair. And the only difference between us is Ricky's out there trying to get even. And he knows not to trust anybody and he got it straight from me. And he knows not to try to get work, and guess where he got that. He walks around like there's loose boards in the floor, and you know who laid that floor, I did.

MAMA: Ricky isn't through yet. You don't know how he'll turn out!

JESSIE: *(Going back to the kitchen)* Yes I do and so did Cecil. Ricky is the two of us together for all time in too small a space. And we're tearing each other apart, like always, inside that boy, and if you don't see it, then you're just blind.

MAMA: Give him time, Jess.

JESSIE: Oh, he'll have plenty of that. Five years for forgery, ten years for armed assault . . .

MAMA: *(Furious)* Stop that!

DICTIONARY WORK

Some of the words and expressions in the scene from *'night, Mother* may be unfamiliar or confusing because they have more than one meaning. Here are dictionary-style definitions of some of these words.

When there is more than one meaning, mark the definition that best fits this passage.

to arm *(verb)*	to supply or fit weapons and armor; prepare for war
assault *(noun)*	violent and sudden attack
board *(noun)*	long, thin, flat piece of wood used in building walls or floors
to dress up *(phrasal verb)*	to put on special clothes, as for fantasy play or a formal occasion
to forge *(verb)*	1. to shape metal by heating and hammering 2. to form or make 3. to make or write falsely, in order to deceive
to get even *(phrasal verb)*	to cause to be (or become) equal
to lay *(verb)*	to put on a surface; place in a lying or resting position
loose *(adj.)*	free; not tight or restrained
manicure *(noun)*	care of the hands and fingernails
to tear *(verb)*	to pull sharply apart or into pieces
valuable *(adj.)*	of great value, worth, or use

COMPREHENSION QUESTIONS

Answer the following questions based on the scene from the play.

1. What does it mean to grow out of something?
2. When Jessie says, "I found it," what is "it"?
3. What does Mama think will happen to Ricky?
4. Does Ricky's mother agree? What does she think will happen to him?
5. What did Ricky steal from his mother?
6. Explain what Mama means when she says, "That's not you're the same person."

POINTS TO CONSIDER AND DISCUSS

1. Why do you think Ricky's grandmother doesn't want him to know that they have a gun in the house?
2. What kind of place do you have to dress up to go to?
3. Do you agree with Mama that we all feel like shooting someone at one time?
4. Which character do you like better? Can you explain why?

VOCABULARY

Complete the following sentences with words from the word list on page 100. You may have to change the form of the word.

1. At Halloween many children like to _____

_____ to go trick-or-treating.

2. Some new immigrants from Asian countries earn a living by

giving _____ .

3. Daisy, when your _____ tooth falls out, put it under

your pillow and the tooth fairy will bring you some money.

4. While Linda was climbing the tree, she _____ a hole in her new shorts.

5. My advice is: Don't get mad; _____ _____.

6. If you had to leave your home suddenly, which _____ things would you take with you?

7. The soldiers made an _____ on the enemy's position.

8. Mr. Stevens told me to buy some three-by-five _____ for the new room.

9. The Whites need to get an expert to help them _____ the carpet.

10. It disturbs me that so many people in this country are _____. I would ban all guns, if I could.

LANGUAGE

Spoken vs. Written Language

Here are some sentences from the play you have just read. They each include examples of spoken English style. Rewrite them in standard, written style. The first sentence is completed as an example.

1. Ricky'll grow out of this and be a real fine boy.
   Ricky will grow out of this and be a really fine boy.

2. It's just something Ricky's going through.

   _____

3. Ricky is as much like me as it's possible for any human to be.

   _____

4. That's just the same size. That's not you're the same person.

   _____

5. We look out at the world and we see the same thing: Not Fair.

_____

6. And the only difference between us is Ricky's out there trying to get even.

_____

Language Chunks

Many students like to learn fixed expressions and use these "chunks of language" in speaking or writing. This kind of learning is very common when you are learning your first language. The characters in this scene use many of these language chunks in their speech.

Here is a list of some of these chunks from the scene we studied. Do you know what they mean? Which ones do you think you could use in your own English?

See how many of these chunks you can find in the second part of the play.

1. . . . grow out of this . . .
2. . . . we had a gun in the house . . .
3. It's just something Ricky's going through.
4. Maybe he's in with some bad people.
5. He just needs some time.
6. He'll get back in school or get a job.
7. . . . he's sorry for all the trouble . . .
8. . . . you've felt like it . . .
9. I hope they put him away . . .
10. I'd turn him in . . .
11. You don't mean that.
12. Every word.

WRITING ACTIVITIES

1. When you were young you might have had a bad habit that your parents objected to. It might have been something like biting your nails or chewing your hair. Explain what the habit was and how you grew out of it. Write an entry in your journal about how you grew out of your bad habit.

2. What should parents do if their own children steal from them? Write a letter to a younger person you know well who has been caught stealing from his or her parents. Give the youth some advice.

3. What do you think happens next in this scene? Write the next part of the scene.

PROSE PASSAGE

Read the following passage.

I.Q.

Do you know what the letters in "I.Q." stand for? In many Western countries children are given a test that is supposed to measure their Intelligence Quotient, or I.Q.

In recent years, many teachers and parents have not been so pleased with I.Q. tests. They say these tests do not measure artistic, musical, social, or athletic abilities, for example. It is also true that these tests do not measure motivation. How people succeed in life very often depends on how motivated they are.

I.Q. tests try to measure the skills that are needed to succeed in school. Your I.Q. may also predict quite well how you will do in terms of jobs and income.

Is a high I.Q. the result of nature or nurture? Some people believe that your I.Q. is a result of nature, the genes you get from your family. Other people believe that your I.Q. comes from nurture, from the care you receive growing up and from your environment.

Nature and nurture seem to be the major influences that make us into the kind of people we are. However, some people are able to overcome both nature and nurture and succeed in the world, even though they are not born into the right family or the right place.

Complete the following sentences in your own words according to the information in the text you read.

1. Your I.Q. measures _____.

2. Some teachers and parents object to I.Q. tests because _____

   _____.

3. When people talk about how smart someone is, they usually

   mean _____.

4. People often succeed in life because _____

   _____.

5. People may not succeed in life because they _____

   _____.

LISTENING TASK

Listen to Susan Sofer, a counselor at a junior high school in California, as she gives advice about teenagers who have gotten into trouble as Ricky has. As you listen, fill in the missing phrases. Each phrase has two or three words.

Question: If you had a student in your school who had been stealing,

   what would you do about it? How/what would you advise the pupil

   (1) _____ _____?

Susan Sofer: I (2) _____ _____ the whole

   family for a meeting. I'd call them (3) _____

   _____ and have them talk about what's

(4) _____ _____ in their lives. Whether this

is the first time (5) _____ _____ something

is going on in the family that (6) _____

_____. And depending on their answer, I would

recommend that they (7) _____ _____ with

more intensive counseling or therapy (8) _____

_____ private therapist who could discuss what is

going on . . . what (9) _____ _____

_____. I'd also want to know if this is, this is a pattern

(10) _____ _____ _____ some-

thing new in this child's life. But, (11) _____

_____, I would recommend that (12) _____

_____ make an effort to go and seek ongoing family

therapy or individual (13) _____.

Q: So you think it's a symptom (14) _____

_____ somebody stealing just because they want

something.

S.S.: It can be (15) _____ _____ or it can also

be a part of teenage rebellion or (16) _____

_____. In that case the family needs to

(17) _____ _____ the fact that the child has

chosen to do this as (18) _____ _____

_____ rebellion.

1. Write down everything you know about Ricky. How old is he? What do you think he looks like? What kind of clothes does he wear? Where do you think he is now? What does he live on if he doesn't work? What does the future hold for Ricky? If you are artistic, draw a picture of Ricky.

2. Act out the scene from the play with a friend or a classmate. If you have a tape recorder or a camcorder, record yourselves. Share your recording with your teacher and class.

3. Find someone who has succeeded in life even though he or she came from a very poor background. Interview the person to try to find out how he or she managed to succeed. Write an article about that person and try to get it published in a school newspaper.

4. Have you ever had or given someone a manicure? Explain what happens during the procedure.

UNIT 10 *Do You Believe in Luck?*

Here are some questions for you to think about and discuss:

Do you believe that there are lucky and unlucky days?

How do most people from your culture feel about this question?

Do you think that these beliefs are changing?

What do you think about horoscopes?

A B O U T   T H E   P L A Y

Most people find it extremely hard to accept the death of one of their children. It may be more difficult to accept the death of a son or daughter in wartime. In recent wars, we have had an added problem: soldiers missing in action. In some cases, one parent accepts that a child who has been missing for many years is dead, while the other parent keeps hoping that the child is alive.

This is the situation in the play *All My Sons,* by Arthur Miller. In this scene, the characters discuss the possibility that Larry Keller was killed in World War II. Joe Keller accepts that his son may be dead, but his wife,

Kate, refuses to believe it. She asks their neighbor, Frank, to find out if November 25 was a lucky day for their son.

Arthur Miller, born in 1915, is one of America's leading playwrights. He was born in New York City and began writing plays while he was a student at the University of Michigan. *All My Sons*, published in 1947, was the first play to bring him great success. Most of Miller's plays are set in the family. They usually deal with political and moral questions.

Read the following scene between Joe Keller, his neighbor Frank, and Jim, the family doctor. Kate is Larry's mother and Keller's wife.

Arthur Miller
from ALL MY SONS

Don't forget to read the stage directions as well as the dialogue.

FRANK: *(Struck)* You know?—it's funny.

KELLER: What?

FRANK: Larry was born in August. He'd been twenty-seven this month. And his tree blows down.

KELLER: *(Touched)* I'm surprised you remember his birthday, Frank. That's nice.

FRANK: Well, I'm working on his horoscope.

KELLER: How can you make him a horoscope? That's for the future, ain't it?

FRANK: Well, what I'm doing is this, see. Larry was reported missing on November 25th, right?

KELLER: Yeah?

FRANK: Well, then, we assume that if he was killed it was on November 25th. Now, what Kate wants . . .

KELLER: Oh, Kate asked you to make a horoscope?

FRANK: Yeah, what she wants to find out is whether November 25th was a favorable day for Larry.

KELLER: What is that, favorable day?

FRANK: Well, a favorable day for a person is a fortunate day, according to his stars. In other words it would be practically impossible for him to have died on his favorable day.

KELLER: Well, was that his favorable day?—November 25th?

FRANK: That's what I'm working on to find out. It takes time! See, the point is, if November 25th was his favorable day, then it's completely possible he's alive somewhere, because . . . I mean it's possible. *(He notices Jim now. Jim is looking at him as though at an idiot. To Jim—with an uncertain laugh)* I didn't even see you.

KELLER: *(To Jim)* Is he talkin' sense?

JIM: Him? He's all right. He's just completely out of his mind, that's all.

FRANK: *(Peeved)* The trouble with you is, you don't *believe* in anything.

JIM: And your trouble is that you believe in *anything*.

DICTIONARY WORK

Some of the words and expressions in the scene from *All My Sons* may be unfamiliar or confusing because they have more than one meaning. Here are dictionary-style definitions of some of these words.

When there is more than one meaning, mark the definition that best fits this passage.

according to *(prep.)*
1. as stated or indicated by; on the authority of
2. in keeping with; in agreement with
3. as determined by

to assume *(verb)*
1. to take upon oneself, as the duties of an office or political power
2. to put on the appearance of; pretend
3. to take for granted; suppose

favorable *(adj.)*
1. advantageous; helpful
2. winning approval; pleasing
3. granting what has been desired or requested

fortunate *(adj.)*	1. bringing something good and unforeseen; auspicious
	2. having unexpected good fortune; lucky
horoscope *(noun)*	1. the positions of the planets and stars at a given moment, such as the time of a person's birth
	2. a diagram of the signs of the zodiac based on such positions
	3. a prediction of personal fortune or characteristics based on the locations of the heavenly bodies at the moment of one's birth
missing *(adj.)*	1. not present; absent, lost
	2. lacking; wanting
practically *(adv.)*	1. in a sensible way
	2. for all reasonable purposes; virtually
	3. all but; nearly; almost
to report *(verb)*	1. to make or present an often official, formal, or regular account
	2. to relate or tell about; present results
	3. to provide an account or summation for publication or broadcast
	4. to carry back and repeat to another
	5. to complain about or denounce

COMPREHENSION QUESTIONS

Answer the following questions based on the scene from the play.

1. When is Larry's birthday?

2. In which month does this scene take place?

3. Why does Keller find it strange that Frank is working on Larry's horoscope?

4. Who asked Frank to make the horoscope? Why?

5. What do Keller and Jim think about horoscopes?

6. What does Jim think about Frank?

7. What is the trouble with Frank, according to Jim?

8. What does Frank think about Jim?

POINTS TO CONSIDER AND DISCUSS

1. Do the characters know if November 25th was a favorable day for Larry?

2. What does the phrase "a favorable day" mean?

3. Is it possible for people to die on their favorable day? Explain.

4. According to the text, Jim questions everything, while Frank believes in everything. Which way do you see things in life?

VOCABULARY

Complete this passage with words from the word list on pages 111–112. You may have to change the form of the word.

PREDICTING THE FUTURE

Many of my students believe in luck. They come from cultures where (1) _____ are considered to be very important. (2) _____ them, they would never get married, buy a house, or go on a long trip without consulting a fortune teller. It's (3) _____ impossible for me to believe in such things. I (4) _____ that this is so because my parents brought me up to be very scientific. My mother warned me never to go to a fortune teller. She (5) _____ that one of her friends was given bad news when her fortune was told. Later she became so depressed that she had to see a psychiatrist. My mother assured me that I would not be (6) _____ anything in life if I avoided fortune tellers.

LANGUAGE

This scene contains many phrase patterns that are typical of spoken English. Rephrase the examples below to make them sound like written English. The first sentence has been done as an example.

1. He'd been twenty-seven this month.

   He would have been twenty-seven this month.

2. That's for the future, ain't it?

   _____

3. Well, what I'm doing is this, see.

   _____

4. Larry was reported missing on November 25th, right?

   _____

5. Oh, Kate asked you to make a horoscope?

   _____

6. What is that, favorable day?

   _____

7. Well, was that his favorable day?—November 25th?

   _____

8. He's just completely out of his mind, that's all.

   _____

WRITING ACTIVITIES

1. Look up your horoscope for today in three different newspapers. Are they the same or different? Compare and contrast the predictions. How do people write horoscopes? What do you think about this subject?

2. Examine the language used in horoscopes. What tense are they written in? Do the writers prefer the active or passive voice? What

about sentence length? Is there a difference in the style of language used in different magazines or newspapers?

PROSE PASSAGE

Read the horoscopes and fill in the gaps with a suitable word.

AQUARIUS   January 21–February 19

You're great at giving advice but not very good at being on the

receiving end, so there's probably no point in telling you

(1) _____ to do. It's a shame because

(2) _____ you were to take a (3) _____

safety measures, you'd probably do (4) _____ well for

yourself this week.

PISCES   February 20–March 20

It's not unusual for any of us to get along better with strangers

than we do with close friends and family. There's tension

(5) _____ your family right now, and

(6) _____ needs to be dealt with rather

(7) _____ just swept under the (8) _____.

ARIES   March 21–April 20

You'll need to make compromises all through this busy week. With

so much to (9) _____, you won't be able to give

(10) _____ much time as you'd (11) _____

to every item on your list. Knowing (12) _____, the idea

of trying to (13) _____ everywhere at once will appeal

the most.

TAURUS   April 21–May 21

Love is still the big issue for you right now. You shouldn't be expect-

ing a wild romance, (14) _____ that isn't what you want

(15) _____ now anyway. It's companionship, comfort,

(16) _____ support that you really

(17) _____.

GEMINI   May 22–June 22

You're really sick of being stuck in the same old rut. If you

(18) _____ to go through the same routine

(19) _____ more time, you're likely to

(20) _____ with frustration. But do try to cheer

(21) _____—there's plenty of light at the

(22) _____ of the tunnel this week.

CANCER   June 23–July 23

Because you're not an island, you can't just decide to do whatever

you want. You have commitments that must be honored and

promises that have to be kept.

LEO   July 24–August 23

Speak clearly and listen carefully this week. You could end up

doing (23) _____ quite unnecessary if you jump to

(24) _____ wrong conclusion. Avoid reading

(25) _____ the lines of what a loved one

(26) _____ saying—and try not to

(27) _____ for any hidden meanings in a simple

statement.

VIRGO August 24–September 23

Life is uncertain at the moment. You're beginning to feel very insecure. But you could be about to get some welcome help from a very surprising source.

LIBRA   September 24–October 23

This week there's a real opportunity to break free from a tiring situation and explore a much more exciting possibility. Try not to see it as any kind of a threat, but treat it as the gift it is. You won't regret taking this chance.

SCORPIO   October 24–November 22

This is a good time for you, so try to make the most of it. Whether you know it or (28) _____, you've got every reason to be pleased with (29) _____ at the moment. A wonderful (30) _____ chapter of your life is all set to begin.

SAGITTARIUS   November 23–December 21

You'll have lots of opportunities to become better off—either by getting a pay raise, learning to economize, or becoming part of a brand-new team.

CAPRICORN   December 22–January 20

You'll hear some news that proves beyond doubt an exciting change is just around the corner if you're ready for it.

Listen to the plot (story) of the play. You will hear it read twice. Mark the following sentences T (true) or F (false). When the answers are false, correct the information.

1. The Kellers live near Columbus, Ohio.
2. The action took place before World War II.
3. Chris Keller is the head of the family.
4. Larry Keller was in the Air Force.
5. Joe Keller is an educated man.
6. Joe Keller has a successful business.
7. The business sold faulty or defective parts to the Air Force.
8. Keller and his partner Deever did not know that the parts were defective.
9. Deever took the blame.
10. Kate Keller is afraid that her husband is guilty.
11. Kate accepts that her son Larry is dead.
12. Kate agrees that her other son Chris will marry Anne Deever.
13. Arthur Miller writes plays that deal with moral problems.
14. Arthur Miller is not interested in parent-child relationships.
15. The neighbors play an important part in *All My Sons*.

SPECIAL ASSIGNMENTS

1. Form groups of three and read the scene from the play. Listen to each other. Try to improve your pronunciation. Notice that words written in italics must be stressed. Make a recording of the scene and listen to it with your group.
2. Write a dialogue between two people. Imagine that one of them believes in horoscopes and the other does not.

3. Find out what you can about Arthur Miller in your library. Write a short biography of him.

4. Do you know anyone whose child was killed in a war? What do they feel about this death? Do they consider that their child was a hero?

UNIT 11   *Job Satisfaction*

INTRODUCTION

Here are some questions for you to think about and discuss:

Many people believe that we each have three main problems to solve in life: where we live; whom we will share our lives with; and what kind of work we will do.

Which problem do you think is the most difficult to solve?

Do you agree that these are our main problems?

What is the best kind of job to have?

Do you know anyone who has a job that you would like to have? Explain.

Do you think that teachers and college professors are usually happy with their careers?

Would you like to teach?

Some people believe that most young people today will have a number of careers during their lifetimes. Do you agree? Can you explain why this might happen?

What would you do if you found that you had made a mistake and hated your job?

ABOUT THE PLAY

A character pours out his frustration with his career in this scene from *La Maison Suspendue*. Michel Tremblay, a French Canadian playwright, won the 1990 Floyd S. Chalmers Canadian Play Award for this play. It was translated into English from French. Its first English production took place in Ontario, Canada, in 1990.

In this scene, you'll hear the voice of Jean-Marc, a forty-eight-year-old professor. He is complaining to his friend Mathieu about his teaching job.

Michel Tremblay
from LA MAISON SUSPENDUE

JEAN-MARC: Up until recently, when I'd see one of my colleagues, a little older than me, get his inevitable but questionable sabbatical, I'd say: "Ah, voilà, another who's found an excuse for living off society for a year!" I'd watch them go off, all smiles, as if their prison door had opened after twenty years of hard labor; at times I'd get a postcard from some place I'd never heard of, at times I'd hear they were just shut up in the house, depressed or paranoid, and, when the year was up, I'd watch them come back more depressed than ever because now they had to start all over again, as if that year had never existed . . . And naively I'd tell myself I'd never do that because I love my profession, because my students inspire me and never in a million years would I need to get away from it all . . . And here I am . . . You begin your career with enthusiasm, you're going to shape people's lives, you have a responsibility . . . If the teachers who preceded you bored their students, you won't make their mistake, non, you will make them passionate because you are passionate yourself! How long does it last, seven, eight years . . . And by sheer repetition, the same things year after year, the same course, you become so sick of it you start hating the students as much as your subject! You don't need to prepare your course anymore, you know it too well, you've *become* your course. You've become the king of bullshit! You look for new ways to say the same goddammed things and there aren't any! You've tried them all! You're like an actor who has played the same part all his life and who ends up hating it. So, before you kill one of your students, or sink into a deep depression, you start dreaming . . . of a year's vacation, at the university's expense because it owes you that much after fifteen or twenty years of playing the trained parrot . . . You've become bitter, nasty, like the older profs you despised when you began . . . I loved my profession so much, Mathieu, and now I hate it with a passion!

DICTIONARY WORK

Some of the words and expressions in the scene from *La Maison Suspendue* may be unfamiliar or confusing because they have more than one meaning. Here are dictionary-style definitions of some of these words.

When there is more than one meaning, mark the definition that best fits this passage.

bitter *(adj.)*
1. tasting sharp and unpleasant
2. unwelcome to the mind; unpleasant; causing sorrow

colleague *(noun)*
person working with another or others

depressed *(adj.)*
1. pressed, pushed, or pulled down; lowered
2. sad; in low spirits
3. made less active

to despise *(verb)*
to feel contempt for; consider unworthy; hate

enthusiasm *(noun)*
strong feeling of admiration or interest

inevitable *(adj.)*
impossible to avoid; sure to happen

to inspire *(verb)*
to put uplifting thoughts, feelings, or aims into something or someone

naive *(adj.)*
natural and innocent in speech and behavior

nasty *(adj.)*
1. dirty; disgusting; unpleasant
2. immoral; indecent
3. unpleasant; disagreeable
4. troublesome; awkward
5. dangerous; bad

paranoia *(noun)*
a mental disorder marked by delusions of persecution or of one's importance

passion *(noun)*
1. strong feeling or emotion, as love, hate, or anger
2. enthusiasm, strong liking

to precede *(verb)*	to come or go before in time, place, or order
questionable *(adj.)*	doubtful, uncertain
responsible *(adj.)*	1. legally or morally in a position where one may be blamed for loss, failure, or injury
	2. having obligations and duties
	3. reliable; trustworthy
sheer *(adj.)*	1. complete; thorough; absolute
	2. finely woven and almost transparent
	3. almost without a slope; straight up and down, as a cliff
to sink *(verb)*	1. to drop below the horizon or a surface such as water
	2. to slope downward; go to the bottom

COMPREHENSION QUESTIONS

Answer the following questions based on the scene from the play.

1. How do professors spend their time when they're on sabbatical, according to the speaker?

2. Describe how some professors behave when they return to the university.

3. How does Jean-Marc think he will react to his sabbatical?

4. How does Jean-Marc feel about his job?

5. How did he feel when he first began to teach?

6. What does Jean-Marc compare professors to?

POINTS TO CONSIDER AND DISCUSS

1. Why does Jean-Marc suggest that sabbaticals are questionable? Why are they inevitable?

2. In what way does a professor "live off society" during the sabbatical?

3. Explain "you've *become* your course."

4. How can professors escape their daily routine?

5. Explain what "a trained parrot" is.

VOCABULARY

Word Families

It may help to think about words having "families." Study this chart and note what the words have in common.

NOUN	VERB	ADJECTIVE	ADVERB
depression	depress	depressing depressed	depressingly
enthusiasm	enthuse	enthusiastic	enthusiastically
inspiration	inspire	inspiring inspired	inspiringly
passion		passionate	passionately
question	question	questionable	questionably

Using the Vocabulary

Complete the following sentences with words from the chart above or the word list on pages 123–124. You may have to change the form of the word.

1. If you believe everything that people tell you, you are truly

   _____.

2. Many psychiatrists prescribe Prozac for their patients who are

   feeling _____.

3. The captain of a ship is _____ for the lives of all the

   passengers.

4. This is a _____ waste of time. There's no hope that we

   can ever succeed. I give up.

5. The mental patient was so _____ that he thought

   everyone wanted to kill him.

6. The person who painted that wonderful picture must have felt

_____.

7. When you don't get a job you wanted very badly, it's hard not to

feel _____.

8. Many students tell me that they had to take _____

medicine when they were sick.

9. Cynthia is _____ about music. She goes to concerts

every week and buys many compact discs.

10. Professor Sherwin didn't believe that Lisa signed this document.

The signature looked _____ to him.

11. That marriage won't last, I'm afraid. Divorce is _____.

LANGUAGE

Many teachers agree that the best way to teach information is to present it to the students in two or three different ways. In the scene we studied, you will notice that Jean-Marc often says the same thing in different ways. An example is: "And by sheer repetition, the same thing year after year. . . ."

Find another way to say the following sentences. Be careful not to change the meaning. The first sentence has been done for you as an example.

1. Young teachers often have more patience with their students than older teachers do.

   Older teachers often have less patience with their students than younger teachers do.

2. When you are a young teacher, you are usually more ready to try out new ideas.

3. Some teachers need a sabbatical to do research.

4. Some teachers take a vacation for a year to write a book.

5. Many teachers on sabbatical leave travel to strange places.

6. Some teachers say that their students inspire them.

7. Certain teachers say they have a responsibility to help shape their students' lives.

8. Some people make a mistake by choosing to be teachers.

WRITING ACTIVITIES

1. Write a dialogue in which a parent gives a child advice about choosing a career.

2. Write a letter to someone who asked you for advice about choosing a career.

3. Prepare an advertisement for a job that you could place in a newspaper or on the Internet. Make sure that you cover such things as salary, conditions, and required experience. Study some examples before you begin.

PROSE PASSAGE

Read the following passage.

PROBLEMS ON THE JOB

. . . I knew I could no longer continue in the teaching profession. To wake in the morning with the fear of the day ahead, to force a hasty breakfast down an unwilling throat, and then to set off for work with pounding heart and frozen face had become habitual, and I had turned to tranquilizers to help me along.

It had not always been as bad as this. Ten years ago I managed well enough, and the holidays for rest and recuperation used to come round just in time.

But I, in common with most other teachers, am enormously self-critical, and I came to realize that I was no longer "managing." My classes were noisy, the children were not learning very much, my attempts to cope with changing teaching methods were patchy, and I had run out of enjoyment and enthusiasm. It was time to stop.

Compare and contrast this teacher's feelings and mood with those of Jean-Marc in the scene from the play.

Some people are very happy with their jobs. Listen to this discussion between Gregory Hatch, an assistant stage manager at the Oregon Shakespeare Festival in Ashland, and an audience that is asking him questions about his work.

Mark the statements Gregory Hatch makes. They may not be in the same words that you hear, but they have the same meaning. Correct statements that are not true.

1. I never went to college. You have to learn to be an assistant stage manager on the job.
2. You don't need a book to do this job.
3. I worked in the theater doing different jobs before I got this one.
4. I'm a very good actor too.
5. I'm in charge of the costumes and props.
6. I make sure that the actors are on stage at the right time.
7. In *Coriolanus,* most of the actors carry books.
8. The director stays with the play all the time.
9. Time and timing are very important; that's why I carry a stopwatch.
10. The stage manager takes over the job when the director leaves the play.
11. Computers are not useful during the process of staging a play.
12. Sometimes actors wear two costumes so that they can change quickly.
13. Children and animals are no problem in a play.
14. When something goes wrong, the play must go on.
15. I would like to be a director in the future.
16. I do not like my job.
17. Being an assistant stage manager is not a difficult job.
18. An assistant stage manager acts as the liaison between the actors and the director.

1. Imagine that you are a news reporter. Using a tape recorder or a camcorder, interview someone who has a job that you would like to have. Record the person for about five minutes. Transcribe the interview and then rewrite it in formal English. Would a newspaper publish your piece? Here are some questions you might ask the person:

   - What kind of work do you do?
   - How did you get this job?
   - Did you have to get special training to get the position?
   - How many hours do you work each week?
   - What do you like best about your job?
   - What do you like least about the job?
   - Does the job pay well?
   - Would you recommend this work to someone else?

2. Read the scene aloud a few times. Remember to pause between ideas. When you see spaced periods, or *ellipsis points,* it means you should pause. Don't read too fast. Make a recording of the speech. Ask your teacher or a friend to comment on your reading.

3. What does the expression "a square peg in a round hole" mean? Do you know anyone who is really unhappy in his or her job? Describe that person's unhappiness and frustration.

4. What kinds of jobs will pay the most in the future? Go to the library or the Internet to find out information.

5. How do most people decide what kind of job to do? Should people follow the profession that their parents suggest? How will or how did you decide on your career? Explain.

UNIT 12   *Which Is More Important— the Past, Present, or Future?*

INTRODUCTION

Here are some questions for you to think about and discuss:

Some people live in the past. They spend most of their time thinking about what used to be. Some people, on the other hand, think mainly about the future.

Which group do you belong to?

What about your parents or older people you know?

Do you have any things in your family that you received from your ancestors? Describe them.

What value do these objects hold for you?

When people leave things to their descendants, how do they decide who should receive them?

Do you think this varies from one culture to another?

A B O U T   T H E   P L A Y

In *The Piano Lesson*, playwright August Wilson deals with one person who cares primarily about the past and another who cares more about the future. This play, first produced in 1988 by the Yale Repertory Theater, won the 1990 Pulitzer Prize for drama.

The title *The Piano Lesson* has two meanings. Can you work out what these two meanings are? The piano in this play is very old—an antique.

It is beautifully hand-carved with scenes from the history of a family whose people were once slaves in Mississippi.

The main conflict in this play is between a brother, Boy Willie, and his sister, Berniece. They inherited the piano from their ancestors. Boy Willie wants to sell the piano and buy some farmland in Mississippi. Berniece wants to keep the piano to remind her of the history of her family.

The dilemma of the piano reminds us of one of the problems of some African Americans. They have very few possessions to remind them of their past.

In this scene, Boy Willie and Berniece argue about the future of the piano. Notice that the two characters do not use standard American English. They speak in B.E.V. (Black English Vernacular).

August Wilson
from THE PIANO LESSON

Don't forget to read the stage directions as well as the dialogue.

BOY WILLIE: Now, I'm gonna tell you the way I see it. The only thing that make that piano worth something is them carvings Papa Willie Boy put on there. That's what make it worth something. That was my great-grandaddy. Papa Boy Charles brought that piano into the house. Now, I'm supposed to build on what they left me. You can't do nothing with that piano sitting up here in the house. That's just like if I let them watermelons sit out there and rot. I'd be a fool. Alright now, if you say to me, Boy Willie, I'm using that piano. I give out lessons on it and that help me make my rent or whatever. Then that be something else. I'd have to go and say, well, Berniece using that piano. She building on it. Let her go on and use it. I got to find another way to get Sutter's land. But Doaker say you ain't touched that piano the whole time it's been up here. So why you wanna stand in my way? See, you just looking at the sentimental value.

See, that's good. That's alright. I take my hat off whenever somebody say my daddy's name. But I ain't gonna be no fool about no sentimental value. You can sit up here and look at the piano for the next hundred years and it's just gonna be a piano. You can't make more than that. Now I want to get Sutter's land with that piano. I get Sutter's land and I can go down and cash in the crop and get my seed. As long as I got the land and the seed then I'm alright. I can always get me a little something else. Cause that land give back to you. I can make me another crop and cash that in. I still got the land and the seed. But that piano don't put out nothing else. You ain't got nothing working for you. Now, the kind of man my daddy was he would have understood that. I'm sorry you can't see it that way. But that's why I'm gonna take that piano out of here and sell it.

BERNIECE: You ain't taking that piano out of my house.

(She crosses to the piano.)

Look at this piano. Look at it. Mama Ola polished this piano with her tears for seventeen years. For seventeen years she rubbed on it till her hands bled. Then she rubbed the blood in . . . mixed it up with the rest of the blood on it. Every day that God breathed life into her body she rubbed and cleaned and polished and prayed over it. "Play something for me, Berniece. Play something for me, Berniece." Every day. "I cleaned it up for you, play something for me, Berniece." You always talking about your daddy but you ain't never stopped to look at what his foolishness cost your mama. Seventeen years' worth of cold nights and an empty bed. For what? For a piano? For a piece of wood? To get even with somebody? I look at you and you're all the same. You, Papa Boy Charles, Wining Boy, Doaker, Crawley . . . you're all alike. All this thieving and killing and thieving and killing. And what it ever lead to? More killing and more thieving. I ain't never seen it come to nothing. People getting burned up. People getting shot. People falling down their wells. It don't never stop.

Some of the words and expressions in the scene from *The Piano Lesson* may be unfamiliar or confusing because they have more than one meaning. Here are dictionary-style definitions of some of these words.

When there is more than one meaning, mark the definition that best fits this passage.

carving *(noun)*   something cut into a desired shape, usually for decoration

crop *(noun)*
1. cultivated plants or agricultural produce, such as grain, vegetables, or fruit
2. the total yield of such produce in a particular season or place
3. a group, quantity, or supply appearing at one time
4. a short haircut

to polish *(verb)*
1. to make smooth and shiny, usually by rubbing
2. to remove the outer layers from grains of rice
3. to free from coarseness; refine
4. to make perfect or complete

to pray *(verb)*
1. to address a prayer to God or another object of worship
2. to make a fervent request or an entreaty

to rot *(verb)*
1. to undergo decomposition, especially organic decomposition; decay
2. to become damaged, weakened, or useless through decay
3. to languish; decline
4. to decay morally; degenerate

seed *(noun)*
1. a ripened plant ovule containing an embryo

2. the propagative part of any plant, from which it can grow
3. seeds considered as a group

sentimental *(adj.)*
1. affectedly or extravagantly emotional
2. colored by emotion rather than reason or reality
3. appealing to the sentiments, especially to romantic feelings

to suppose *(verb)*
1. to assume to be true or real for the sake of argument or explanation
2. to believe, especially on uncertain or tentative grounds
3. to consider to be probable or likely
4. to imply as an antecedent condition; presuppose
5. to consider as a suggestion

thief *(noun)*
one who steals, especially one who steals movable property by stealth rather than force

COMPREHENSION QUESTIONS

Answer the following questions based on the scene from the play.

1. Who did the carvings on the piano?
2. How is the carver related to Berniece and Boy Willie?
3. Does Berniece actually use the piano? Does she play the piano?
4. Why does Boy Willie want to sell the piano? What does he plan to do with the money?
5. Why does Berniece want to keep the piano?
6. According to Boy Willie, would his father have agreed to his selling the piano?
7. How did Mama Ola take care of the piano?
8. What does Berniece say about the men in her family?

1. How does Boy Willie plan to farm the land that he wants to buy from Sutter?

2. Why do you think that Berniece refuses to sell the piano?

3. Who is right about the piano? Berniece? Boy Willie? Why?

4. In some cultures, only sons inherit property from their families. In other cultures, property is divided up equally among the children. What happens in the cultures that you know about?

VOCABULARY

Complete the following sentences with words from the word list on pages 134–135. You may have to change the form of the word.

1. I have some silver spoons that belonged to my great-grandparents. They have great _____ value for me.

2. Last year some _____ stole my silver, but luckily the police got it back.

3. Aladdin had to _____ the lamp to make the genie appear.

4. When people are afraid, they often _____ to God to help them.

5. Now that you have won all that money, I _____ you'll stop working.

6. When we visited the Egyptian pyramids, we were impressed by the _____ of people and animals on the walls.

7. It's been raining for days. I'm afraid that the vegetables in the garden are going to _____.

8. I want to plant some sweetpea _____, but I think I'll wait until it stops raining.

9. If the birds don't get to them first, we'll have a good _____ of apricots.

LANGUAGE

There is very little difference in the written English we study in schools in various places. There are, however, great differences in the way people speak English. We usually call these different kinds of spoken English *dialects*. One of the most interesting dialects in English is called B.E.V.—Black English Vernacular. In this scene from *The Piano Lesson*, the two characters speak in B.E.V. Berniece and Boy Willie are black Americans who are descended from slaves. If you study this kind of language, you will note some interesting patterns.

Here are some spoken English sentences from the scene. Change each one into standard written English. The first sentence has been completed as an example.

1. The only thing that make that piano worth something is them carvings.

   The only thing that makes that piano worth something are those carvings.

2. You can't do nothing with that piano sitting up here in the house.

3. Then that be something else.

4. I'd have to go and say, well, Berniece using that piano.

5. That's alright.

6. You ain't got nothing working for you.

7. You ain't taking that piano out of my house.

8. You always talking about your daddy but you ain't never stopped to look at what his foolishness cost your mama.

9. And what it ever lead to?

10. It don't never stop.

1. Write to a close relative who owns something that you really value. Explain why you love it.

2. Describe Mama Ola's marriage based on the facts you are given in the scene.

3. If you inherited a lot of money, what would you do with it? Write your answer in your journal.

PROSE PASSAGE

In her book *The Color Purple*, Alice Walker gives readers some information about Africa and African Americans. Here is an extract from a letter written by Nettie to her sister Celie. Nettie and her friends, all African Americans, have just arrived in Africa.

Read this passage from **The Color Purple.**

Did you know there were great cities in Africa, greater than Milledgeville or even Atlanta, thousands of years ago? That the Egyptians who built the pyramids and enslaved the Israelites were colored? That Egypt is in Africa? That the Ethiopia we read about in the Bible meant all of Africa?

Well, I read and I read until I thought my eyes would fall out. I read where the Africans sold us because they loved money more than their own sisters and brothers. How we came to America in ships. How we were made to work.

I hadn't realized I was so *ignorant*, Celie. The little I knew about my own self wouldn't have filled a thimble! And to think Miss Beasley always said I was the smartest child she ever taught! But one thing I do thank her for, for teaching me to learn for myself, by reading and studying and writing a clear hand. . . .

Think what it means that Ethiopia is Africa. All the Ethiopians in the bible were colored. It had never occurred to me, though when you read the bible it is perfectly plain if you pay attention only to the words. It is the pictures in the bible that fool you. The pictures that illustrate the words. All of the people are white and so you think all the people from the bible were white too. But really *white* white people lived somewhere else during those times. That's why the bible says that Jesus Christ had hair like lamb's wool. Lamb's wool is not straight, Celie. It isn't even curly.

Answer the following questions based on the passage.

1. What do you know about the Egyptians?
2. Why did some Africans sell their brothers and sisters?
3. How did the Africans who were sold get to America?
4. What happened to them in America?
5. What is wrong with the pictures in the Bible, according to Nettie?
6. What did Jesus Christ look like?

SPECIAL ASSIGNMENTS

1. With a classmate, act out the scene from the play. Try to tape yourselves and listen to the recording.
2. Find out what you can about August Wilson in the library or the Internet. Try to find a picture of him. Write a short biography of this playwright.
3. If you are interested in language, go to the library to find out about Black English Vernacular. Report your findings to the class.

UNIT 13 *Arranging a Marriage*

INTRODUCTION

Here are some questions for you to think about and discuss:

One of the major differences among cultures is the way marriages are arranged. In most Western countries, young people expect and prefer to find their own husbands or wives. In many other cultures, parents normally arrange their children's marriages.

How do young people find their husbands and wives in the cultures you know about?

What do you know about the way that marriages happen in the country where you live now?

Are there any differences from what you are used to?

Is it normal in your home culture for the mother to interview a young man who wants to marry her daughter?

A B O U T   T H E   P L A Y

Oscar Wilde was born in Dublin, Ireland, in 1854 and died in 1900. It's important to realize that he was making fun of people who were overly serious. The absurdities of courtship and matchmaking are exposed in Wilde's 1895 farce, *The Importance of Being Earnest*.

In this scene from *The Importance of Being Earnest*, Lady Bracknell interviews a young man named Jack, who wants to marry her daughter, Gwendolen. The young couple have found each other—but before they get married, they have to receive Lady Bracknell's permission.

Oscar Wilde
from THE IMPORTANCE OF BEING EARNEST

Don't forget to read the stage directions as well as the dialogue.

LADY BRACKNELL: *(Sitting down)* You can take a seat, Mr. Worthing.
　　　(Looks in her pocket for notebook and pencil)
JACK: Thank you, Lady Bracknell, I prefer standing.
LADY BRACKNELL: *(Pencil and notebook in hand)* I feel bound to tell you
　　　that you are not down on my list of eligible young men, although
　　　I have the same list as the dear Duchess of Bolton has. We work
　　　together, in fact. However, I am quite ready to enter your name,
　　　should your answers be what a really affectionate mother requires.
　　　Do you smoke?
JACK: Well, yes, I must admit I smoke.
LADY BRACKNELL: I am glad to hear it. A man should always have an
　　　occupation of some kind. There are far too many idle men in Lon-
　　　don as it is. How old are you?
JACK: Twenty-nine.
LADY BRACKNELL: A very good age to be married at. I have always been of
　　　the opinion that a man who desires to get married should know
　　　everything or nothing. Which do you know?
JACK: *(After some hesitation)* I know nothing, Lady Bracknell.
LADY BRACKNELL: I am pleased to hear it. I do not approve of anything
　　　that tampers with natural ignorance. Ignorance is like a delicate
　　　exotic fruit; touch it and the bloom is gone. The whole theory of
　　　modern education is radically unsound. Fortunately in England, at
　　　any rate, education produces no effect whatsoever. If it did, it

would prove a serious danger to the upper classes, and probably lead to acts of violence in Grosvenor Square. What is your income?

JACK: Between seven and eight thousand a year.

LADY BRACKNELL: *(Makes a note in her book)* In land, or in investments?

JACK: In investments, chiefly.

LADY BRACKNELL: That is satisfactory. What between the duties expected of one during one's lifetime, and the duties exacted from one after one's death, land has ceased to be either a profit or a pleasure. It gives one position, and prevents one from keeping it up. That's all that can be said about land.

JACK: I have a country house with some land, of course, attached to it, about fifteen hundred acres, I believe; but I don't depend on that for my real income. In fact, as far as I can make out, the poachers are the only people who make anything out of it.

LADY BRACKNELL: A country house! How many bedrooms? Well, that point can be cleared up afterwards. You have a town house, I hope? A girl with a simple, unspoiled nature, like Gwendolen, could hardly be expected to reside in the country.

JACK: Well, I own a house in Belgrave Square, but it is let by the year to Lady Bloxham. Of course, I can get it back whenever I like, at six months' notice.

LADY BRACKNELL: Lady Bloxham? I don't know her.

JACK: Oh, she goes about very little. She is a lady considerably advanced in years.

LADY BRACKNELL: Ah, nowadays that is no guarantee of respectability of character. What number in Belgrave Square?

JACK: 149.

LADY BRACKNELL: *(Shaking her head)* The unfashionable side. I thought there was something. However, that could easily be altered.

JACK: Do you mean the fashion, or the side?

LADY BRACKNELL: *(Sternly)* Both, if necessary, I presume. What are your politics?

JACK: Well, I am afraid I really have none. I am a Liberal Unionist.

LADY BRACKNELL: Oh, they count as Tories. They dine with us. Or come in the evening, at any rate. Now to minor matters. Are your parents living?

JACK: I have lost both my parents.

LADY BRACKNELL: Both? . . . That seems like carelessness. Who was your father? He was evidently a man of some wealth. Was he born in what the Radical papers call the purple of commerce, or did he rise from the ranks of the aristocracy?

JACK: I am afraid I really don't know. The fact is, Lady Bracknell, I said I had lost my parents. It would be nearer the truth to say that my parents seem to have lost me . . . I don't actually know who I am by birth. I was . . . well, I was found.

LADY BRACKNELL: Found!

JACK: The late Mr. Thomas Cardew, an old gentleman of a very charitable and kindly disposition, found me, and gave me the name of Worthing, because he happened to have a first-class ticket for Worthing in his pocket at the time. Worthing is a place in Sussex. It is a seaside resort.

LADY BRACKNELL: Where did the charitable gentleman who had a first-class ticket for this seaside resort find you?

JACK: (Gravely) In a hand-bag.

LADY BRACKNELL: A hand-bag?

JACK: (Very seriously) Yes, Lady Bracknell. I was in a hand-bag—a somewhat large, black leather hand-bag, with handles to it—an ordinary hand-bag in fact.

LADY BRACKNELL: In what locality did this Mr. James, or Thomas, Cardew come across this ordinary hand-bag?

JACK: In the cloak-room at Victoria Station. It was given to him in mistake for his own.

LADY BRACKNELL: The cloak-room at Victoria Station?

JACK: Yes. The Brighton line.

LADY BRACKNELL: The line is immaterial. Mr. Worthing, I confess I feel somewhat bewildered by what you have just told me. To be born, or at any rate bred, in a hand-bag, whether it had handles or not, seems to me to display a contempt for the ordinary decencies of family life that remind one of the worst excesses of the French Revolution. And I presume you know what that unfortunate movement led to? As for the particular locality in which the hand-bag was found, a cloak-room at a railway station might serve to conceal a social indiscretion—has probably, indeed, been used for that purpose before now—but it could hardly be regarded as an assured basis for a recognized position in good society.

JACK: May I ask you then what you would advise me to do? I need hardly say I would do anything in the world to insure Gwendolen's happiness.

LADY BRACKNELL: I would strongly advise you, Mr. Worthing, to try and acquire some relations as soon as possible, and to make a definite effort to produce at any rate one parent, of either sex, before the season is quite over.

JACK: Well, I don't see how I could possibly manage to do that. I can produce the hand-bag at any moment. It is in my dressing-room at home. I really think that should satisfy you, Lady Bracknell.

LADY BRACKNELL: Me, sir! What has it to do with me? You can hardly imagine that I and Lord Bracknell would dream of allowing our only daughter—a girl brought up with the utmost care—to marry into a cloak-room, and form an alliance with a parcel? Good morning, Mr. Worthing! *(She sweeps out in majestic indignation.)*

JACK: Good morning!

DICTIONARY WORK

Some of the words and expressions in the scene from *The Importance of Being Earnest* may be unfamiliar or confusing because they have more than one meaning. Here are dictionary-style definitions of some of these words.

When there is more than one meaning, mark the definition that best fits this passage.

advanced *(adj.)*
1. highly developed or complex
2. at a higher level than others
3. ahead of the times; progressive
4. far along in course or time

affection *(noun)*

1. a tender feeling toward another; fondness
2. a moderate feeling or emotion
3. a disposition to feel, do, or say; a propensity

alliance *(noun)*

1. a close association formed to advance common interests or causes
2. a formal agreement establishing such an association, especially an international treaty of friendship
3. a connection based on kinship, marriage, or common interest; a bond or tie
4. a close similarity in nature or type; affinity

aristocracy *(noun)*

1. a hereditary ruling class; nobility
2. government by a ruling class or by a small group of citizens considered to be best qualified to lead
3. a state or country having this form of government
4. a group or class considered superior to others

to bind *(verb)*

1. to tie or secure, as with a rope or cord
2. to bandage
3. to hold or restrain with or as if with bonds
4. to compel or obligate
5. to unite or fasten together

to breed *(verb)*

1. to produce offspring
2. to originate and thrive

charitable *(adj.)*

1. generous in giving money or other help to the needy

	2. mild or tolerant in judging others; lenient
	3. concerned with charity
considerable *(adj.)*	1. large in amount, extent, or degree
	2. worthy of consideration; significant
contempt *(noun)*	1. disdain for something base or unworthy; scorn
	2. the state of being despised or dishonored; disgrace
	3. open disrespect for or disobedience of authority, especially of a court of law
discretion *(noun)*	1. the quality of being discreet; circumspection
	2. ability or power to decide responsibly
	3. freedom to act or judge on one's own
disposition *(noun)*	1. one's usual mood; temperament
	2. habitual inclination; tendency
	3. arrangement or distribution
	4. a final settlement
	5. a bestowal or transfer to another
eligible *(adj.)*	1. qualified or entitled
	2. desirable and worthy of choice, especially for marriage
to exact *(verb)*	1. to force the payment or yielding of; extort
	2. to demand and obtain by force or authority
excess *(noun)*	1. an amount or quantity beyond what is normal or sufficient; surplus
	2. the amount or degree by which one quantity exceeds another
	3. intemperance; overindulgence
	4. behavior or action that exceeds proper or lawful bounds

exotic *(adj.)*	1. from another part of the world; foreign
	2. intriguingly unusual or different; excitingly strange
handle *(noun)*	1. a part designed to be held or operated with the hand
	2. an opportunity or means for achieving a purpose
idle *(adj.)*	1. not employed or busy
	2. avoiding work or employment; lazy
	3. not in use or operation
	4. lacking substance, value, or basis
ignorance *(noun)*	lack of knowledge, training, or information
investment *(noun)*	1. the act of investing
	2. an amount invested
	3. property or another possession acquired for future financial return or benefit
	4. a commitment, as of time or support
locality *(noun)*	a particular neighborhood, place, or district
particular *(adj.)*	1. associated with a specific person, group, thing, or category; not general or universal
	2. separate and distinct from others of the same group, category, or nature
	3. worthy of note; exceptional
to presume *(verb)*	1. to take for granted as being true
	2. to give reasonable evidence for assuming; appear to prove
	3. to venture without authority or permission; dare

radical *(adj.)*	1. arising from or going to a root or source; basic
	2. departing markedly from the usual or customary; extreme
to reside *(verb)*	1. to live in a place permanently or for an extended period
	2. to be inherently present; exist
	3. to be vested, as a power or right
respectable *(adj.)*	1. meriting respect or esteem; worthy
	2. properly behaved
	3. of moderately good quality
	4. considerable in amount, number, or size
	5. acceptable in appearance; presentable
to tamper *(verb)*	1. to interfere in a harmful manner
	2. to tinker with rashly or foolishly
	3. to engage in improper or secret dealings, as in an effort to influence

COMPREHENSION QUESTIONS

Answer the following questions based on the scene from the play.

1. Is Jack on Lady Bracknell's list of men who would be eligible to marry her daughter? Explain.

2. How does Lady Bracknell feel about the fact that Jack smokes?

3. What does she think about his age?

4. When Jack says that he knows nothing, how does Lady Bracknell react?

5. What does she think about British education?

6. How does Jack describe his financial situation?

7. How does Lady Bracknell feel about owning land?

8. What kind of character does Gwendolen have, according to Lady Bracknell?

9. What happened to Jack's parents?

10. Does Jack know who his parents were? Explain.

11. Who found Jack? Where? How did he get his family name?

12. What does Lady Bracknell advise Jack to do?

POINTS TO CONSIDER AND DISCUSS

1. Why doesn't Jack want to sit down when Lady Bracknell invites him to do so?

2. When Lady Bracknell tells Jack that she has the same list as Duchess Bolton has, what does that tell us?

3. Do you believe Jack when he says he knows nothing? What does he mean?

4. Jack says his income is between seven and eight thousand a year. Is that enough for Lady Bracknell?

5. Why does Lady Bracknell say that her daughter would not be able to live in the country?

6. What does Lady Bracknell mean when she says that 149 Belgrave Square is on the unfashionable side?

7. Do you think that the Bracknells will allow Gwendolen to marry Jack?

8. Many people think that this scene is very funny. What makes it humorous?

VOCABULARY

Complete the following sentences with words from the word list on pages 145–149. You may have to change the form of the word.

1. When I met Daniel, he seemed highly _____; but then I saw the wedding ring on his finger.

2. Sometimes people sign a letter to a close friend or relative "_____ yours."

3. Don't listen to _____ gossip about friends. Usually it's not true.

4. Many Americans think that a mango is an _____ fruit.

5. My father lost all his money by making bad _____.

6. That passport is fake; you can see that someone _____ with it.

7. Do you trust politicians who have _____ opinions? I prefer people who are more conservative.

8. The employment form asks where you _____. Why don't they just ask for your address?

9. My granddaughter can read at age four. Don't you think she's _____ for her age?

10. When the explorer Stanley met Livingstone in Africa, people believe that he said: "Dr. Livingstone, I _____?"

11. If you are a duke or a duchess, you are a member of the _____.

12. I have a lot of respect for _____ people who give money to others who need help.

13. Do you know where I can find someone to fix the broken _____ on my suitcase?

14. Did you have a _____ perfume for your wife in mind, or will any one do?

15. It's sad when people feel _____ for others just because they are different.

LANGUAGE

When we read this scene today, we notice that some of the language is rather formal and old-fashioned.

Read the following sentences from the play and mark those that you think are old-fashioned. Then change those sentences into modern spoken English. The first sentence has been completed as an example.

1. She is a lady considerably advanced in years.

   She is an old (elderly) lady.

2. I prefer standing.

3. Do you smoke?

4. I do not approve of anything that tampers with natural ignorance.

5. What is your income?

6. That's all that can be said about land.

7. Well, I am afraid I really have none.

8. I have lost both my parents.

9. I was found.

10. In what locality did this Mr. Cardew come across this ordinary hand-bag?

11. It was given to him in mistake for his own.

12. I need hardly say I would do anything in the world to insure Gwendolen's happiness.

WRITING ACTIVITIES

1. Make a list of the advantages and disadvantages of an arranged marriage. Write an essay or give a talk to your class about your results.

2. Write a letter to someone close to you in which you explain why he or she should (or should not) marry at this time.

3. Write a dialogue between a father and a young man who wants to marry his daughter.

SPECIAL ASSIGNMENTS

1. Study the scene from the play with a friend or a classmate. Once you feel confident that you know your parts, act out the scene. If you have access to a camcorder, videotape yourselves.

2. This play is still very popular. If possible, go with your class to see a performance of it. You should also be able to find the play on video to enjoy with your class.

UNIT 14 *The Greatest Person Who Ever Lived*

INTRODUCTION

Here are some questions for you to think about and discuss:

Who do you think was the greatest person who ever lived? Why?

Do you think you would choose a different person if you came from another country?

How should younger people treat older people?

Does it make any difference if the older people are servants?

How do you learn the right way to treat people?

What do you know about the racial situation in South Africa today?

Has it changed recently?

What was life like for black people in the South in the U.S. in the 1950s?

A B O U T   T H E   P L A Y

In his play *"Master Harold" . . . and the Boys,* Athol Fugard includes a scene in which two of the characters debate over who was the greatest person who ever lived. Fugard was born in South Africa in 1932. Most of his plays are about racial problems. This play was first produced in 1982 at the Yale Repertory Theater.

In order to understand this scene better, go to the library and find out about some of these famous people: Athol Fugard, Napoleon, Charles Darwin, Abraham Lincoln, William Wilberforce, William Shakespeare, Leo Nikolaevich Tolstoy, Winston Churchill, Jesus Christ, Mohammed, Sigmund Freud, Socrates, Alexandre Dumas, Karl Marx, Dostoevsky, Nietzsche, and Alexander Fleming. It might be a good idea to do this research in groups. Share what you find with your class. Try to find photographs or paintings of these people.

"Master Harold" . . . and the Boys contains three characters: Hally, a seventeen-year-old white boy, and Willie and Sam, black men in their mid-forties. They work for Hally's mother in a tearoom in Port Elizabeth, South Africa. The play is set in the 1950s.

In this scene from Fugard's play, we hear the voices of Hally and Sam. Because Sam has had no opportunity to be educated, Hally teaches him what he learns in school.

Athol Fugard
from "MASTER HAROLD" . . . AND THE BOYS

Don't forget to read the stage directions as well as the dialogue.

HALLY: I don't know about him [Napoleon] as a man of magnitude.

SAM: Then who would you say was?

HALLY: To answer that, we need a definition of greatness, and I suppose that would be somebody who . . . somebody who benefited all mankind.

SAM: Right. But like who?

HALLY: *(He speaks with total conviction.)* Charles Darwin. Remember him? That big book from the library. *The Origin of the Species.*

SAM: Him?

HALLY: Yes. For his Theory of Evolution.

SAM: You didn't finish it.

HALLY: I ran out of time. I didn't finish it because my two weeks was up. But I'm going to take it out again after I've digested what I read. It's safe. I've hidden it away in the Theology section. Nobody ever goes in there. And anyway who are you to talk? You hardly even looked at it.

SAM: I tried. I looked at the chapters in the beginning and I saw one called "The Struggle for an Existence." Ah ha, I thought. At last! But what did I get? Something called the mistletoe which needs the apple tree and there's too many seeds and all are going to die except one . . . ! No, Hally.

HALLY: *(Intellectually outraged)* What do you mean, No! The poor man had to start somewhere. For God's sake, Sam, he revolutionized science. Now we know.

SAM: What?

HALLY: Where we come from and what it all means.

SAM: And that's a benefit to mankind? Anyway, I still don't believe it.

HALLY: God, you're impossible. I showed it to you in black and white.

SAM: Doesn't mean I got to believe it.

HALLY: It's the likes of you that kept the Inquisition in business. It's called bigotry. Anyway, that's my man of magnitude. Charles Darwin! Who's yours?

SAM: *(Without hesitation)* Abraham Lincoln.

HALLY: I might have guessed as much. Don't get sentimental, Sam. You've never been a slave, you know. And anyway we freed your ancestors here in South Africa long before the Americans. But if you want to thank somebody on their behalf, do it to Mr. William Wilberforce. Come on. Try again. I want a real genius. *(Now enjoying himself, and so is Sam. Hally goes behind the counter and helps himself to a chocolate.)*

SAM: William Shakespeare.

HALLY: *(No enthusiasm)* Oh. So you're also one of them, are you? You're basing that opinion on only one play, you know. You've only read my *Julius Caesar* and even I don't understand half of what they're talking about. They should do what they did with the old Bible: bring the language up to date.

SAM: That's all you've got. It's also the only one *you've* read.

HALLY: I know. I admit it. That's why I suggest we reserve our judgment until we've checked up on a few others. I've got a feeling, though, that by the end of this year one is going to be enough for me, and I can give you the names of twenty-nine other chaps in the Standard Nine class of the Port Elizabeth Technical College who feel the same. But if you want him, you can have him. My turn now. *(Pacing)* This is a damned good exercise, you know! It started off looking like a simple question and here it's got us really probing into the intellectual heritage of our civilization.

SAM: So who is it going to be?

HALLY: My next man . . . and he gets the title on two scores: social reform and literary genius . . . is Leo Nikolaevich Tolstoy.

SAM: That Russian.

HALLY: Correct. Remember the picture of him I showed you?

SAM: With the long beard.

HALLY: *(Trying to look like Tolstoy)* And those burning, visionary eyes. My God, the face of a social prophet if ever I saw one! And remember my words when I showed it to you? Here's a *man*, Sam!

SAM: Those were words, Hally.

HALLY: Not many intellectuals are prepared to shovel manure with the peasants and then go home and write a "little book" called *War and Peace*. Incidentally, Sam, he was somebody else who, to quote, ". . . did not distinguish himself scholastically."

SAM: Meaning?

HALLY: He was also no good at school.

SAM: Like you and Winston Churchill.

HALLY: *(Mirthlessly)* Ha, ha, ha.

SAM: *(Simultaneously)* Ha, ha, ha.

HALLY: Don't get clever, Sam. That man freed his serfs of his own free will.

SAM: No argument. He was a somebody, all right. I accept him.

HALLY: I'm sure Count Tolstoy will be very pleased to hear that. Your turn. Shoot. *(Another chocolate from behind the counter)* I'm waiting, Sam.

SAM: I've got him.

HALLY: Good. Submit your candidate for examination.

SAM: Jesus.

HALLY: *(Stopped dead in his tracks)* Who?

SAM: Jesus Christ.

HALLY: Oh, come on, Sam!

SAM: The Messiah.

HALLY: Ja, but still . . . No, Sam. Don't let's get started on religion. We'll just spend the whole afternoon arguing again. Suppose I turn around and say Mohammed?

SAM: All right.

HALLY: You can't have them both on the same list!

SAM: Why not? You like Mohammed, I like Jesus.

HALLY: I *don't* like Mohammed. I never have. I was merely being hypo-
thetical. As far as I'm concerned, the Koran is as bad as the Bible.
No. Religion is out! I'm not going to waste my time again arguing
with you about the existence of God. You know perfectly well I'm
an atheist . . . and I've got homework to do.

SAM: Okay, I take him back.

HALLY: You've got time for one more name.

SAM: *(After thought)* I've got one I know we'll agree on. A simple
straightforward great Man of Magnitude . . . and no arguments.
And *he* really *did* benefit all mankind.

HALLY: I wonder. After your last contribution I'm beginning to doubt
whether anything in the way of an intellectual agreement is
possible between the two of us. Who is he?

SAM: Guess.

HALLY: Socrates? Alexandre Dumas? Karl Marx? Dostoevsky? Nietzsche?

(Sam shakes his head after each name.)

Give me a clue.

SAM: The letter P is important . . .

HALLY: Plato!

SAM: . . . and his name begins with an F.

HALLY: I've got it. Freud and Psychology.

SAM: No. I didn't understand him.

HALLY: That makes two of us.

SAM: Think of moldy apricot jam.

HALLY: *(After a delighted laugh)* Penicillin and Sir Alexander Fleming!
And the title of the book: *The Microbe Hunters. (Delighted)*
Splendid, Sam! Splendid. For once we are in total agreement. The
major breakthrough in medical science in the Twentieth Century. If
it wasn't for him, we might have lost the Second World War. It's
deeply gratifying, Sam, to know that I haven't been wasting my
time in talking to you. *(Strutting around proudly)* Tolstoy may have
educated his peasants, but I've educated you.

Some of the words and expressions in the scene from *"Master Harold"*
. . . and the Boys may be unfamiliar or confusing because they have more
than one meaning. Here are dictionary-style definitions of some of these
words.

When there is more than one meaning, mark the definition that best
fits this passage.

atheist *(noun)* — person who believes there is no God

to base *(verb)* — to use as a basis for

to benefit *(verb)*
1. to do good to someone or something
2. to get help or advantage from a person or situation

bigot *(noun)* — person who stubbornly and unreasonably holds an opinion or belief and is intolerant of the views of others

to digest *(verb)*
1. to break down food in the stomach and bowels so that it can be used by the body
2. to take into the mind; to reduce to order so as to make part of one's knowledge

genius *(noun)*
1. great and exceptional capacity of mind or imagination
2. person having this capacity

to gratify *(verb)*
1. to give pleasure or satisfaction
2. to give something that is desired

heritage *(noun)* — something given or received from ancestors of past generations

hypothesis *(noun)* — idea or suggestion put forward as a starting point for an argument or explanation

incidentally *(adv.)* — by chance, by the way

intellect *(noun)*	power of the mind to reason, as contrasted with feeling and instinct
magnitude *(noun)*	1. size 2. greatness of size or importance 3. comparative brightness of stars
mold *(noun)*	furry growth or fungus that appears on decaying matter, such as cheese or fruit
probe *(noun)*	1. slender instrument used by doctors for investigating the depth and direction of a wound 2. investigation
prophet *(noun)*	1. person whose religious teachings are claimed to come directly from God 2. pioneer of a new theory or cause 3. person who tells or claims to tell what will happen in the future
to reform *(verb)*	to make or become better by removing or correcting what is bad or wrong
to reserve *(verb)*	to store or keep back for a later occasion or special use
revolution *(noun)*	1. act of revolving or going around in a circle 2. complete turn of a wheel or other circular object 3. sudden complete change, as in a political system
serf *(noun)*	person who works on the land and is sold with it like a slave
struggle *(noun)*	fight or great effort

COMPREHENSION QUESTIONS

Answer the following questions based on the scene from the play.

1. Find examples of language in the text to demonstrate that Hally and Sam treat each other as equals; for instance, they use each other's first names.

2. Find some expressions in the text to show that Sam and Hally are having a friendly argument. For example, when Sam agrees with Hally, he says, "No argument." When Hally disagrees with Sam, he says, "You can't have them both on the same list."

3. Find passages in the text to show that Hally thinks he is better than Sam. For example, when they are talking about Shakespeare, Hally says: "Even I don't understand half of what they're talking about."

4. When Sam says, "It's the only one *you've* read," why is the word "you've" printed in italics?

5. Whom does Hally finally choose as his Man of Magnitude? Whom does Sam choose?

6. Why is Hally so pleased with Sam's final idea?

POINTS TO CONSIDER AND DISCUSS

1. Hally is still a schoolboy and Sam is a middle-aged man, but most of the time they seem to talk to each other as equals. Can you explain why?

2. Why do you think that Sam mentions Abraham Lincoln?

3. Why doesn't Hally offer Sam a chocolate when he takes one himself?

4. What was Sam thinking when he saw the title of Darwin's chapter "The Struggle for an Existence"? Explain what Sam was referring to.

5. Hally says, "I suggest we reserve our judgment until we've checked up on a few others." Why are Hally and Sam not ready to accept other people's ideas about greatness?

6. Do you think the two characters have discussed religion before? How do you know?

7. Fugard's play is called *"Master Harold" . . . and the Boys.* Can you explain the punctuation of the title?

VOCABULARY

Complete the following sentences with words from the word list on pages 160–161. You may have to change the form of the word.

1. Do you think we can eat this cheese? It looks a bit

   _____.

2. It helps to succeed in higher education if you are an

   _____.

3. Some foods are _____ more easily than others.

4. The taxes you pay are _____ on the money you earn.

5. Ms. Smith is not looking well. I think she would _____

   from a vacation.

6. Einstein was one of the greatest _____ of this century.

7. We need to _____ these seats for our special guests.

8. In many countries, people have to _____ to make a

   living.

In the scene we studied, Hally and Sam agree and disagree with each other. See how many examples of agreement and disagreement you can find. Here are a few examples:

Agreement	Disagreement
a. Like you and Winston Churchill.	a. Oh, come on, Sam.
b. That makes two of us.	b. Anyway, I still don't believe it.

Read the following statements and then write a response that agrees or disagrees with each one. Try to use some of the expressions you studied in the play. Three responses to the first statement have been provided for you as examples.

1. It's freezing cold today.
   I agree.
   That's true.
   I'm not cold.

2. Lovely weather, isn't it?

3. The Forty-Niners are the best team.

4. She shouldn't be allowed to go to the Olympics.

5. Smoking should be banned in all public places.

6. Fathers should share responsibilities for children and housework.

7 Teachers should earn more money than doctors and engineers.

8. Mothers should not go out to work. They should stay at home with their children

WRITING ACTIVITIES

1. Hally and Sam do not mention the names of famous women. Write about a woman you consider to be great.

2. Write the next scene of the play in your own words. What do you think will happen next?

3. Write in your journal about your reactions to this scene from the play.

SPECIAL ASSIGNMENTS

1. Read the play aloud with a partner. After you have critiqued each other's performance, present the scene in front of the class. Pay attention to body language, pronunciation, and intonation. Try to dress appropriately for your parts and have some real props. If you can, make a recording of the performance.

2. Give a three-minute speech about the famous person you admire most. It does not have to be someone already mentioned in this unit.

3. Go to the library to find out information about Athol Fugard. Write a biography of this playwright.

4. If you were born and educated in another country, do you agree with Sam and Hally's list of famous people? Whom on the list have you heard of before? Make a list of people who are famous in the country you come from. What makes them special?

5. South Africa has changed a great deal since this play was written. Go to the library or the Internet to find out about South Africa today.

A P P E N D I X

To the Instructor

The grammar section of *The Play's the Thing* deals only with grammatical items that appear in the context of the scenes from the plays. In some cases, the explanations are detailed because they are relevant for several units. In other cases, the explanations are brief and can be supplemented with additional material from other sources.

It is preferable that you first try, by looking at the examples, to elicit any grammatical rules and explanations from the students themselves.

Depending on the level of your class, you may find some of these grammar units more useful than others. They may be used both for direct teaching and for review.

Some of the exercises refer back to items focused on in previous units. This enables the students to reinforce the material already taught in the context of the plays.

UNIT 1

Present Simple Tense

The scene from the play contains many examples of sentences spoken in the *present simple tense:*

The snow **falls** in winter.

Winter **is** one of the four seasons.

I **beg** your pardon.

We use the present simple tense to talk about:

habits and routine

a permanent situation

facts that are always true

Note: In the third person singular *(he, she, it)*, we add *-s* to the verb in the present simple tense:

The sun **rises** in the East and **sets** in the West.

He **plays** tennis on Sundays.

Find some more examples of sentences in the present simple tense in the scene from the play. Write them down.

Present Continuous (Progressive) Tense

In the scene there are also a few examples of the *present continuous (progressive) tense:*

It**'s** not **raining** and it**'s** not **snowing** either.

We use the present continuous tense to talk about things that are happening right now, at the moment of speaking. We also use it to talk about incomplete actions.

Find some more examples in the scene from the play and write them down.

Circle the correct verb form given in the parentheses.

1. My sister always *(study / is studying / studies)* hard for exams.
2. I have a test next week so I *(am studying / studies / study)* hard.
3. We generally *(are eating / eat / eats)* breakfast before we *(leave / are leaving / leaves)* for work in the morning.
4. Look! It *(rains / rain / is raining)* and everyone *(is running / runs / run)* for shelter.
5. Suzie *(play / plays / is playing)* the piano well, but it is her sister Betty who *(is playing / plays / play)* now.

Match phrases from the two columns to form complete correct sentences.

1. I study French and Arabic   a. until I start college.
2. I'm studying French   b. by bus.
3. She does   c. for an important exam.
4. She's taking   d. in her boutique.
5. He uses a computer   e. with very good teachers.

6. He's using a pencil   f. the laundry on Mondays.

7. We go there   g. by bus today.

8. We are going there   h. to draw that picture.

9. I work for my mother   i. an art course at the university.

10. I'm working for my mother   j. at work.

Question Forms

There are three different ways of asking questions used in the scene from the play:

using *intonation*—"I expect that you are the new pupil**?**"

using *tag questions*—"You will excuse me, **won't you?**"

using a *question structure*—"**Did you have** any trouble finding the house?"

Find some more examples of these three types of questions in the text.

When we ask a question by using *intonation,* we make our voice rise toward the end of the sentence. When someone hears the rising tone of our voice, he or she understands that we are asking a question, not making a statement.

We can form a question by adding a *tag question* to the end of a sentence. We use this type of question to check if the information is correct or to ask for agreement. The tag question is formed by adding a helping verb that agrees with the verb in the sentence plus a pronoun that stands for the subject.

You can come to my party, **can't you?**

She will bake a cake, **won't she?**

He likes rock music, **doesn't he?**

The most common way to ask a question is by changing the word order into *question structure.* To ask a question whose answer is yes or no in the present simple or past simple tense, we use the helping verbs *do, does,* or *did* followed by the subject and the base form of the verb. (*Exception:* When the verb is *be,* do not use a helping verb.)

Do you **live** here?   **Does** she **sing** well?

Are you happy?   **Was** he very angry?

With tenses that use a helping verb, we use the first helping verb at the beginning to form the question.

> **Has** the train **arrived** yet?

> **Had** he **been speaking** for long when we got there?

> **Will** you **come** if you're invited?

When we want to ask questions about people, things, time, or place, we use the yes/no question form and add a *WH-* word to the beginning of the question. The *WH-* words are: *who, which, what, when, why, where,* and others like *how long* or *how much/many.*

> **How long** will it take us to get there?

> **Where** should I meet you?

> **When** do they close the stores?

Change the following questions to another question form.

1. Do you like baseball?
2. This party is fun, isn't it?
3. You know everyone here?
4. Have you eaten anything?
5. You'd like a lift home?
6. Sharon's a wonderful hostess, isn't she?
7. People aren't leaving already, are they?
8. Will you be coming to Ben's party next week?

Use some of the questions to create part of a dialogue. Complete the dialogue with suitable answers.

UNIT 2

Past Tense

Here are some examples of sentences in the *past tense* in the scene from the play:

> When Mom **could** finally bring me to the U.S., I **was** already ten.

> But I never **studied** my English very hard in Taiwan.

Find some more examples of sentences in the past tense in the text.

We use the past tense when we want to talk about events or actions that took place at a definite time in the past.

Sometimes when a whole passage or paragraph is about things that happened in the past, there is no need for time expressions to tell us when they happened. However, there are some common time expressions that we use with the past tense: *last week / month / year, yesterday,* phrases with the word *ago* (a year **ago**), and phrases beginning with *when* (**when** I **was** a child).

The regular past tense is formed by adding -*ed* to the verb.

If the verb ends in -*y*, we change the *y* to *i* and then add -*ed*.

If the verb ends in *e*, just add -*d*.

There are many irregular verbs in English; you will need to learn their special forms.

Match phrases from the two columns to form complete correct sentences.

1. We played football	a. so she didn't come for a week.
2. She walks to school	b. in 1969.
3. The teacher was ill	c. at school social events.
4. Man first walked on the moon	d. until midnight last night.
5. She plays the piano	e. a week ago.
6. They watched TV	f. when her bike is broken.
7. I visited him	g. when he ran a red light.
8. He crashed his car	h. last winter.

How many of the sentences are in the present simple tense? How many are in the past simple?

Circle the correct verb form given in parentheses.

1. I *(be / am / was)* very unhappy when I first *(arrive / arrived / arriving)* here.

2. It *(take / was take / took)* me a long time to learn the language.

3. I *(had / have / has)* many lessons with a private teacher.

4. My family *(makes / make / made)* friends with our new neighbors, who *(were / was / is)* very kind and helpful.

5. When we finally *(buy / bought / buys)* our own apartment we really *(begin / beginning / began)* to feel at home.

6. We soon *(forgot / forget / forgets)* about the difficult beginnings.

UNIT 3

Past Tense: "Used to" and "Used"

Here are two sentences with the expressions *"used to"* or *"used"* from the scene in this unit:

My mother **used to** make me Jello.

Well, the formula I've **used** has always worked.

Here are some more examples (not from the play):

People **used to** travel by ship, but now they travel more by plane.

It's better to **use** your money wisely than to waste it.

You'll **get used to** the new car with all its gadgets.

I **am used to** hard work. It doesn't bother me.

When we want to talk about something that generally, always, or repeatedly happened in the past, we use the verb phrase *used to:*

She **used to** live here. (But she doesn't anymore.)

When we want to describe things that we are (or are becoming) accustomed to, we use the form *to be used to* or *to get used to*. If this phrase is followed by a verb, the second verb takes the gerund form:

She **is used to getting** up early.

Fill in the correct form of the expressions *use, used to,* or *be/get used to,* according to the meaning of the sentence.

1. He _____ my pen and then forgot to return it to me.

2. She's not very reliable; I _____ her coming late.

3. I _____ visit them until they moved away.

4. Many mothers _____ formula for their babies, and the babies _____ drinking it.

5. He _____ smoke a pipe, but he's given up smoking altogether.

6. Everything was new and different on my first day at work, but eventually I _____ it.

7. Some people _____ eating regularly in restaurants.

8. She _____ a special wax to polish the floors.

Questions Review

Refer back to the question forms in Unit 1. Find questions in the scene from the play in Unit 3. Note that tag questions are not used. Rewrite or ask the questions, using an alternative form.

Present Perfect Tense

Here are some sentences from the play spoken in the *present perfect tense:*

> Well, the formula I**'ve used has** always **worked**.

> They**'ve been** around for years and you know they work.

Here are some more examples (not from the play):

> He **has lived** here for ten years.

> I **have** always **eaten** fresh food.

> She **has** already **cooked** dinner.

> We **have owned** this restaurant since 1990.

We use the present perfect tense to talk about:

> a past event whose exact time of occurrence is not important or not known

> actions begun in the past that are not yet completed

> a situation or fact that began in the past and is still relevant and true

We form the present perfect tense by using the helping verb *have / has* with the past participle, or third form, of the verb. The third form of regular verbs is formed by adding *-ed* to the verb. Check what the third forms of irregular verbs are.

Circle the correct verb form given in parentheses.

1. She *(seen / has seen / is seeing)* that movie twice already.

2. I'm not hungry; I *(have eaten / eat / am eating)* dinner.

3. They *(are living / live / have lived)* here for five years.

4. That famous author *(writing / has written / writes)* ten books.

5. We like this hotel very much. We *(stay / are staying / have stayed)* here many times.

6. Did you see her run? I think she *(breaks / is breaking / has broken)* the world record.

7. He *(has been / is / were)* late for every meeting so far.

8. I can't wait for Ben's surprise party. We *(prepare / has prepared / have prepared)* many exciting things for it.

UNIT 4

Future Tense

Here are some sentences in the *future tense* from the play:

We **will use** things once.

Then, we **will discard** it.

We **will make** a call on the telephone.

We use the future tense when we talk about events, actions, or situations that we know will take place at some time in the future. We form the *active future tense* by adding the helping verb *will* to the base, or first form, of the verb.

Some examples of the future tense used in the scene in this unit describe actions that we will perform in the future. Other examples describe what will be done to things in the future. This is the *future passive* form. The future passive is formed by adding *will be* to the past participle, or third form, of the verb:

Soon everything **will be used** only once.

A radio or any machine or appliance **will be discarded**.

A new one **will be delivered**.

For a fuller explanation of the passive form, see Unit 10.

Here are some more examples of the future tense from the Prose Passage section of this unit:

> In the future, there **will be** fewer people in the family.

> Some families **will be "chosen"** to have the children.

Complete the following passage, using suitable verb forms from the following list:

will be destroyed	will have	will be eaten
will visit	will spend	will be done
will happen	will consist	

Because no one can really see into the future, everyone has a different picture of how it will look. Some people think we (1) _____ more time in space. They think we (2) _____ other planets. Other people believe that our meals (3) _____ of pills, not real food. Obviously, such meals (4) _____ at home and not in restaurants. All our work and shopping (5) _____ from our home computers, and it seems we (6) _____ lots of free time. There are many pessimistic people who are afraid that the world (7) _____ either by pollution or another disaster. There are so many ideas about the future, I'm sure some of them (8) _____ in reality. We'll just have to wait and see.

UNIT 5

Pay special attention to the question forms in the dialogue of the scene in this unit.

Review of Tenses

The dialogue between Gus and Ben contains many examples of the present simple, present continuous (progressive), past simple, present perfect, and future simple tenses. See how many examples of each structure you can find.

UNIT 6

More on the Future Tense

The future tense was introduced in Unit 4. Here are some more sentences using the future tense, taken from the scene in this unit:

Sometimes I think about what **I'll be doing** five years from now.

Sometimes I think about what your life **will be** like, if Mount Saint Helens **will erupt** again.

What you**'ll become** if you**'ll study** penmanship or word processing.

These examples use both the full form *will* and the contracted form *'ll*. Also note the use of the future progressive form.

Circle the correct verb form given in parentheses.

1. I'm sure that when you grow up you *(be / will be / was)* famous.
2. Don't get there too early. They *(will be eating / will eat / have eaten)* their dinner.
3. I'm learning a lot in this course. In a few weeks I *(was speaking / am speaking / will be speaking)* like a native.
4. She's taking a course in Spanish that *(will finish / has finished / finish)* at the end of next month.
5. They are planning a new bridge over the highway. They *(built / are building / will build)* it next year.

UNIT 7

Negatives

Here are some examples of sentences in *negative form* from the scene in this unit:

Don't do that.

I know, but I **don't** want to do it all the time.

I **won't** marry you but you've talked me into it.

I **wasn't** kidding.

I **can't** resist myself.

Find some more examples in the scene from the play.

These negative forms are contractions (shortened forms) of the helping verb, or modal (see Unit 8), and the negative *not*. To form the negative in the present simple and past simple tenses, we add the helping verbs *do* or *does* (present) or *did* (past) and *not*. All the other tenses have helping verbs, so we just add *not*.

Here are some more examples (not from the play):

I **couldn't** find it.

They **weren't** there.

She **won't** look again.

You **shouldn't** expect miracles.

You **mustn't** forget next time.

Answer the following questions with a suitable negative answer from the examples above.

1. Where's that diary?

   _____

2. Why don't you ask Betty to look for it?

   _____

3. Did you find the pictures I put with the diary?

   _____

4. Why can't I remember where I put things?

   _____

5. Maybe it'll turn up unexpectedly.

   _____

UNIT 8

Modals

Here are some sentences from the scene in this unit containing *modals:*

May I introduce you?

She's mad to come under some really clever man who **can** teach her even more.

She came here as quickly as she **could**.

It's quite likely I **may** be able to find some job for you.

Oh, how **can** I ever thank you?

Modals, unlike other verbs, do not describe actions. We use them to express our attitude toward the action of the verb that comes after the modal. By using the modal, we say whether we think this action is possible, uncertain, advisable, necessary, or whatever else we feel about it:

Here is a list of modals and what they mean.

can/could	present or past ability
	permission
	possibility
	request
	suggestion
should	advice
	opinion
would	polite offer or request
	conditional possibility
may/might	permission
	polite request
	possibility
must	obligation
	strong necessity
	certainty
	persuasion

The following examples (not from the play) show how the modal expresses the speaker's attitude:

It's raining; you **should** take an umbrella.	(It's **advisable.**)
We **must** be more careful next time.	(It's **necessary.**)
He's late. He **might** have missed the bus.	(It's **possible.**)
You **may** sit down.	(It's **permitted.**)

Read the following sentences and write what the modals mean, as in the examples above.

1. It's not a difficult job. Do you think you can do it?

   _____

2. May I have another cup of coffee? _____

3. It's a good idea. You should do it. _____

4. You must get that important report in on time. _____

5. Wait a little longer. She might be on the next bus.

   _____

6. Try again. You can do it. _____

7. May I leave early? _____

8. Would you mind opening the window? _____

9. They're not here. They must have forgotten to meet us.

   _____

10. You look tired. You should take a holiday. _____

Complete the following sentences using a suitable modal.

1. It's hot outside. We _____ stay at home.

2. This is a nonsmoking area. You _____ not smoke here.

3. He missed an important meeting. He _____ be ill.

4. She took a computer course last year. Now she _____
   use her computer for many purposes.

5. Will you come to my party?

   I _____ come. I'm not sure.

6. I would like to help you, but I don't think I _____.

7. We _____ have done it, if more people had helped.

8. These CD's look really interesting.

   You _____ borrow them, if you like.

9. You _____ come on time or you'll miss the train.

10. _____ you like some more coffee?

Adjectives

Here are some expressions containing adjectives from the scene in this
unit:

   a **childhood** friend

   in **earlier** days

a **lucky** moment

some really **clever** man

a **little** something

that shouldn't be **impossible**

Complete the following sentences with one of the adjectives in the examples above.

1. Your excuses are of _____ interest to me.

2. That's a very _____ plan. It should work out well.

3. I remember those stories and games well. They are part of my _____ memories.

4. I'm not sure that I can do that, but it shouldn't be _____.

5. You won the lottery! It must be your _____ day.

UNIT 9

Language Chunks

Two mothers are chatting. One mother disapproves of her daughter's behavior and is complaining to her friend. Make up suitable responses using some of the language chunks in Unit 9.

1. It's 11 o'clock and she's still asleep! She'll drive me mad!

   _____

2. I wish she'd do her schoolwork without my telling her all the time.

   _____

3. She stays out late, goes to wild parties, and never tells me anything.

   _____

4. If this goes on much longer, I'll ground her.

   _____

5. Maybe you'd do a better job as her mother.

   _____

Passive Form

Here are some sentences using the *passive form* from the scene in this unit:

> Larry **was born** in August.
>
> Larry **was reported** missing on November 25.
>
> We assume that if he **was killed** it was on November 25.

These are examples of the *passive form* in the past tense. The future passive form was introduced in Unit 4. The passive form can be used with all tenses. Here are some more examples (not from the play):

> Help! Police! My bag **has been stolen**.
>
> Important decisions **will be made** at the meeting next week.
>
> By the time I got there, a suspect **had been arrested**.
>
> That tree is broken. It **could have been knocked down** by the storm.

We use the passive form when we want to emphasize *what happened* rather than *who did it*. We may not know who does the action, or it may not be important. If it is, we put this information (the doer of the action) at the end of the sentence, preceded by the word *by*:

> This house was designed **by a famous architect**.

The passive form uses the helping verb *be* in the correct tense for the content of the sentence. That is, if we want to talk about something that will happen in the future, we use the future form of the passive (*will be* + past participle). We use the past form (*was / were* + past participle) to describe something that happened in the past.

Circle the correct verb form given in parentheses.

1. That window *(broke / is broken / will be broken)*. How did it happen?

2. Yes, sir. Your parcel *(is delivered / are delivered / has been delivered)*.

3. Our guests are late! The meal *(was ruined / is being ruined / is ruining)*.

4. Have you read this book? It *(was written / will write / was being written)* by a famous writer.

5. By the time I arrived at the party, the food *(had served / had been served / will be served)* and I was hungry.

6. Did you hear about the accident? Several people *(killed / has killed / were killed)*.

7. When I arrived at the hotel, the room I had reserved *(was being cleaned / has cleaned / is being cleaned)*.

8. The scenery in that movie is fantastic! Did you know it *(filmed / was filmed / has filmed)* in Norway?

Match the following sentences in order to make logical pairs.

1. I won't clean that room again.	a. She was very rude at the party.
2. That was a very serious accident.	b. They have both been eaten.
3. I won't speak to her again.	c. It was cleaned yesterday.
4. I baked two cakes yesterday.	d. It was caused by a drunk driver.
5. Children love to play with toys.	e. He's being questioned by the police.
6. He has been arrested.	f. It does not matter if they are old and broken.
7. Football can be dangerous.	g. I hope it has been planned for safety.
8. A new pool is being built in this area.	h. I broke my leg twice playing it.

Which of the above sentences are phrased in the active voice? Which use the passive?

Pronouns

Here are some sentences containing *pronouns* from the scene in this unit:

I'd watch **them** go off, all smiles, as if **their** prison door had opened after twenty years.

You won't make **their** mistake.

I loved **my** profession so much.

A pronoun is a word we use to take the place of a noun or noun phrase in a sentence. The pronoun can be used instead of the subject or the object of the sentence, as long as it is clear what the pronoun refers to:

The man was very kind to my family. **He** helped **us** a lot.

We use *possessive pronouns* to explain whom something or someone belongs to. Possessive pronouns come in front of the noun that is possessed:

This is **my** book.

Sometimes the possessed object is not named together with the pronoun. In this case, the pronoun usually takes a different form:

That book is **mine**.

Reflexive pronouns are used to indicate that the action refers back to the subject of the sentence. That is, the person who performs the action is the same one who "receives" the action:

He washed **himself**.

We also use reflexive pronouns to stress that the action was done only by the subject of the sentence and no one else:

They built it **themselves**.

Here are some sentences from the scenes in Units 11–14. Notice that the pronouns have been stressed.

Unit 11

I'd watch **them** go off, all smiles, as if **their** prison door had opened after 20 years.

You won't make **their** mistake.

I loved **my** profession so much.

Unit 12

I'm gonna tell **you** the way **I** see **it.**

That was **my** great-grandaddy.

Let **her** go on and use **it.**

Unit 13

I feel bound to tell **you** that **you** are not down on **my** list of eligible young men.

We work together, in fact.

I am quite ready to enter **your** name.

Unit 14

I don't know about **him** as a man of magnitude.

So **you**'re also one of **them,** are **you?**

Find some more examples of pronouns in the scene from this unit.

The following chart shows you the different types of pronouns.

	SUBJECT	OBJECT	POSSESSIVE WITH NOUN	POSSESSIVE WITHOUT NOUN	REFLEXIVE
Singular 1st person	I	me	my	mine	myself
Singular 2nd person	you	you	your	yours	yourself
Singular 3rd person	he, she, it	him, her, it	his, her, its	his, hers, its	himself, herself, itself
Plural 1st person	we	us	our	ours	ourselves
Plural 2nd person	you	you	your	yours	yourselves
Plural 3rd person	they	them	their	theirs	themselves

Use the examples and the chart to help you complete the following exercises.

Circle the correct pronoun in parentheses to complete the following passage.

This house has been in the family for many years. (1) *(You, We, Them)* have lived here for as long as (2) *(I, you, they)* can remember. (3) (You, She, I) think (4) *(his, your, my)* grandfather built the house when (5) *(she, me, he)* married (6) *(his, my, I)* grandmother. Grandfather even built some of the house by (7) *(ourselves, herself, himself)*. (8) *(They, We, Them)* had four children who had a very happy childhood in the house. Nowadays, when the family gets together for family celebrations, (9) *(he, it, we)* have lots of room to enjoy (10) *(yourselves, ourselves, themselves)* in the big house and garden.

Fill in the blank spaces with a suitable pronoun.

1. A friend of _____ asked if _____ could borrow _____ car, so _____ lent _____ to _____. However, _____ had a serious accident with the car, and _____ was badly damaged.

2. _____ parents are wonderful people. When _____ celebrated _____ anniversary, _____ made a party for _____ and invited all _____ friends.

3. Everyone forgets things sometimes. However, _____ memory seems to be getting worse, so _____ write things down on pieces of paper. Unfortunately, _____ don't always remember where _____ put _____.

Cohesion/Anaphora

There are a number of ways in which we connect ideas in an English text. One of these is called *anaphora*. This involves replacing a word or group of words that has already been mentioned with a grammatical substitute, for example, a pronoun (see the section on pronouns). We can look back in the text for the referent.

Here is an example from the beginning of the scene from the play:

> Up until recently, when I'd see one of my colleagues . . . get his inevitable . . . sabbatical. . . ."

In this sentence *his* refers to the phrase *one of my colleagues.*

Find the referent for the following anaphoric references in the text:

1. "another" (line 3)
2. "them" (line 4)
3. "they" (line 6)
4. "them" (line 8)
5. "it" all (line 12)
6. "their" mistake (line 15)
7. "them" passionate (line 16)
8. "it" (line 19)
9. "them" (line 23)
10. "it" (line 25)
11. "it" (line 27)
12. "it" (line 30)

UNIT 12

Synonyms and Antonyms

Here are some examples of *synonyms* in the scenes from the plays:

sabbatical—year's vacation	glad—pleased
hate—despise	magnitude—greatness
worth—value	judgment—opinion
rubbed—polished	

Here are some examples of *antonyms* in the scenes from the plays:

love—hate	argument—agreement
lost—found	

Often, when we speak or write, we repeat ideas to stress what we are saying. To do this, we use different words or expressions with the same or similar meanings. Words that have the same meaning or are close in meaning are called *synonyms.* Words that are opposite in meaning are called *antonyms.*

Fill in the blank spaces in the following sentences by choosing suitable words from the examples of synonyms and antonyms above.

1. I was happy to receive a phone call from the man who had _____ the money that I'd _____.

2. You asked me what I think about the situation. Well, that's my _____ of the matter.

3. This jewelry is an imitation. It has little _____.

4. They were _____ to hear the good news.

5. He _____ animals, so he has lots of pets—cats, dogs, and birds.

6. The football players had an _____ with the referee about his decision.

7. I _____ people who listen in to my telephone conversations with others.

8. He's not teaching at college this year. He's taken a _____.

9. She _____ the surface of the table until it looked like new.

UNIT 13

Articles

Here are some examples of *articles* in the scene from the play:

You can take **a** seat. (Any seat, not a specific one.)

I have **the** same list as **the** dear Duchess of Bolton has. (A specific list; the duchess is a specific person.)

A man should always have **an** occupation of some kind.

I was in **a** hand-bag . . . **an** ordinary hand-bag in fact.

Articles do not exist in every language. In English, there are two articles.

The definite article *the* is used to refer to something specific or something that has been mentioned before:

There's **the** man we met yesterday.

The indefinite article *a* or *an* is used when we are not referring to anyone or anything specific or when we are introducing the subject for the first time:

I would like **a** cup of coffee with **a** spoonful of sugar.

The article, definite or indefinite, comes before a noun or before the adjective that describes the noun. If the word (noun or adjective) following the indefinite article begins with a vowel *(a, e, i, o, u)* or a vowel sound, we use *an*, not *a:*

This is **an** umbrella—**an** unusual umbrella, not **an** ordinary one.

The indefinite article is only used before a singular noun. Leave it out before a plural noun:

Umbrellas and raincoats are useful in rainy weather.

Find some more sentences with articles in the scene from the play and write them down.

Fill in the blank spaces with a suitable article: *the, a,* or *an.* Leave the space blank if no article is appropriate.

1. I read _____ interesting article in _____ newspaper today.
2. My mother baked _____ cakes for _____ party this evening.
3. I know _____ artist who painted _____ picture hanging on _____ wall.
4. There is _____ saying in English: "_____ apple _____ day keeps _____ doctor away."
5. I watched _____ exciting movie on TV last night.
6. If you need to write down _____ telephone message, you will need _____ pencil and paper.
7. Most people shop at _____ supermarket where _____ prices are cheaper and there is more variety.
8. I would like you to come to _____ movies with me.

Ellipsis

Here is an example of *ellipsis* in the scene from the play in this unit:

HALLY: I don't know about him as a man of magnitude.

SAM: Then who would you say was [**a man of magnitude**]?

Ellipsis is a grammatical feature of English in which some elements of a sentence are left out because they are found elsewhere in the text. We understand what is being referred to without its being stated again because it has already been mentioned. In the example above, after the word *was,* we mentally refer to *a man of magnitude* from the previous sentence.

Find the person or thing being referred to in the following examples of ellipsis from the scene in this unit.

1. But like who? (line 6)

2. Now we know. (line 24)

3. Who's yours? (line 32)

4. It's also the only one *you've* read. (line 47)

5. We've checked up on a few others. (line 49)

6. One is going to be enough for me. (line 50)

7. Here's a *man,* Sam! (line 65)

8. That makes two of us. (line 116)